# MAN
# FACTS

MAN FACTS

An Hachette UK Company
www.hachette.co.uk

Summersdale Publishers Ltd
Part of Octopus Publishing Group Limited
Carmelite House
50 Victoria Embankment
LONDON
EC4Y 0DZ
UK

www.summersdale.com

Printed and bound in the Czech Republic

ISBN: 978-1-84953-985-2

Substantial discounts on bulk quantities of Summersdale books are available to corporations, professional associations and other organisations. For details contact general enquiries: telephone: +44 (0) 1243 771107 or email: enquiries@summersdale.com.

# MAN
# FACTS

Fascinating things
every bloke
should know

**Dan Bridges**

summersdale

# CONTENTS

ANIMALS 7

ART AND ARTISTS 21

COMPUTER SCIENCE 29

ENGINEERING AND INVENTIONS 38

FILM 56

FOOD AND DRINK 68

HISTORY 84

LANGUAGE 99

LITERATURE 109

MUSIC 125

THE NATURAL WORLD 143

PLACES 164

POLITICS 175

SCIENCE AND MEDICINE 182

SPACE AND ASTRONOMY 195

SPORT 201

THEATRE 241

TRAVEL 252

# A NOTE ON THE FACTS

Every effort has been made to ensure that the
information in this book is correct at the time
of going to press. Inevitably, some facts and
rankings are likely to change over time.

# ANIMALS

# THE WORLD'S LARGEST EVER...

| RODENT | Capybara (South America) | 65 kg / 1.3 m |
|---|---|---|
| LAND MAMMAL | Paraceratherium* (Europe and Central Asia) | 20 t / 5.5 m tall |
| SEA MAMMAL | Blue whale | 80 t / 33 m |
| MARSUPIAL | Diprotodon* (Australia) | 2.7 t / 3 m |
| INSECT | Meganeura* (Europe) | 75 cm (wingspan) |

\* Now extinct

# TOP TEN WORLD'S BIGGEST ANIMALS ON LAND

| 1 | African elephant | 8.5 t / 6.66 m (21.85 ft) |
|---|---|---|
| 2 | Asian elephant | 4.2 t / 5.94 m (19.5 ft) |
| 3 | White rhinoceros | 2.3 t / 3.78 m (12.5 ft) |
| 4 | Hippopotamus | 2.5 t / 3.35 m (11 ft) |
| 5 | Gaur | 1.6 t / 2.99 m (9.8 ft) |
| 6 | Giraffe | 1.4 t / 4.69 m (15.4 ft) |
| 7 | Black rhinoceros | 1.2 t / 3.43 m (11.25 ft) |
| 8 | Walrus | 1.2 t / 3.35 m (11 ft) |
| 9 | Saltwater crocodile | 785 kg / 6.10 m (20 ft) |
| 10 | Wild Asian water buffalo | 770 kg / 3.47 m (11.4 ft) |

# TOP TEN WORLD'S FASTEST ANIMALS ON LAND

| 1 | Cheetah | 71 mph (114 km/h) |
|---|---|---|
| 2 | Pronghorn antelope | 57 mph (95 km/h) |
| =3 | Blue wildebeest | 50 mph (80 km/h) |
| =3 | Lion | 50 mph (80 km/h) |
| =3 | Springbok | 50 mph (80 km/h) |
| =6 | Brown hare | 48 mph (77 km/h) |
| =6 | Red fox | 48 mph (77 km/h) |
| =8 | Grant's gazelle | 47 mph (76 km/h) |
| =8 | Thomson's gazelle | 47 mph (76 km/h) |
| 10 | Horse | 45 mph (72 km/h) |

# TOP TEN WORLD'S FASTEST ANIMALS IN WATER

| 1 | Black marlin | 80 mph (129 km/h) |
|---|---|---|
| 2 | Sailfish | 70 mph (113 km/h) |
| 3 | Mako shark | 60 mph (97 km/h) |
| 4 | Striped marlin | 50 mph (80 km/h) |
| =5 | Killer whale | 48 mph (77 km/h) |
| =5 | Wahoo | 48 mph (77 km/h) |
| 7 | Tunny | 46 mph (74 km/h) |
| 8 | Bluefish tuna | 44 mph (70 km/h) |
| 9 | Blue shark | 43 mph (69 km/h) |
| 10 | Swordfish | 40 mph (64 km/h) |

# TOP TEN WORLD'S FASTEST ANIMALS IN THE AIR

| 1 | Peregrine falcon | 200 mph (322 km/h)* |
|---|---|---|
| 2 | Spine-tailed swift (also known as the white-throated needletail) | 106 mph (171 km/h) |
| 3 | Frigate bird | 95 mph (153 km/h) |
| 4 | Spur-winged goose | 88 mph (142 km/h) |
| 5 | Red-breasted merganser | 80 mph (129 km/h) |
| 6 | White-rumped swift | 77 mph (124 km/h) |
| 7 | Canvasback duck | 72 mph (116 km/h) |
| 8 | Eider duck | 70 mph (113 km/h) |
| 9 | Teal | 68 mph (109 km/h) |
| 10 | Mallard | 65 mph (105 km/h) |

* This speed is achieved only through diving

# TOP TEN WORLD'S BIGGEST BIRDS (AVERAGE WINGSPAN)

| =1 | Albatross | 3.6 m (11.8 ft) |
|---|---|---|
| =1 | Great white pelican | 3.6 m (11.8 ft) |
| 3 | Marabou stork | 3.4 m (11.2 ft) |
| 4 | Andean condor | 3.2 m (10.5 ft) |
| 5 | Bearded vulture | 3 m (9.8 ft) |
| 6 | Whooper swan | 2.99 m (9.8 ft) |
| =7 | Griffon vulture | 2.8 m (9.2 ft) |
| =7 | California condor | 2.8 m (9.2 ft) |
| =9 | Grey crowned crane | 2.5 m (8.2 ft) |
| =9 | Golden eagle | 2.5 m (8.2 ft) |

## Fascinating Facts

- Peregrine falcons are the fastest animals in the world. They fly at an average speed of 90 mph (145 km/h).

- An elephant, despite its ponderous appearance, can reach speeds of up to 25 mph (40 km/h) on an open stretch.

- Sloths move so slowly that algae is formed on their fur – this is advantageous as it serves as camouflage and provides nutrients for the sloth to lick off.

 **COLLECTIVE NOUNS**

| | | | |
|---|---|---|---|
| **Apes** | Shrewdness | **Larks** | Exultation |
| **Baboons** | Congress | **Leopards** | Leap |
| **Bears** | Sleuth | **Mice** | Mischief |
| **Butterflies** | Rabble | **Owls** | Parliament |
| **Cobras** | Quiver | **Penguins** | Huddle |
| **Doves** | Piteousness | **Rattlesnakes** | Rhumba |
| **Eagles** | Convocation | **Ravens** | Unkindness |
| **Emus** | Mob | **Rhinoceroses** | Crash |
| **Ferrets** | Business | **Rooks** | Storytelling |
| **Hawks** | Kettle | **Starlings** | Murmuration |
| **Lapwings** | Deceit | **Weasels** | Sneak |

# TOP TEN WORLD'S DEADLIEST ANIMALS

| | NAME | APPROX. NO. OF DEATHS PER YEAR |
|---|---|---|
| 1 | **Mosquito** | **2–3 million** |
| 2 | Tsetse fly | 250,000 |
| 3 | Snake | 125,000 |
| 4 | Dog (rabies) | 25,000 |
| 5 | Scorpion | 3,500 |
| 6 | Saltwater crocodile | 1,000 |
| 7 | Hippopotamus | 500 |
| 8 | Cape buffalo | 300 |
| 9 | Lion | 100 |
| =9 | Elephant | 100 |

## Fascinating Facts

- A cockroach can survive without its head; entomologist Christopher Tipping decapitated cockroaches under a microscope and a couple lasted for several weeks in a jar.

- Many birds migrate, but the Arctic tern travels furthest. It flies from the Arctic to the Antarctic and back again each year – a round trip of about 32,000 km.

- The iguana can survive in exceptionally high temperatures. Conversely, a thick layer of blubber provides polar bears with such excellent insulation that their body temperature and metabolic rate remain the same, even at −37°C.

MAN FACTS

# ANIMALS' ABODES

| | | | | |
|---|---|---|---|---|
| **Badger** | sett, earth | | **Lion** | den, lair |
| **Bear** | lair, den | | **Mole** | fortress |
| **Beaver** | lodge | | **Otter** | holt |
| **Bee** | hive, apiary | | **Rabbit** | burrow, warren |
| **Eagle** | eyrie | | **Squirrel** | drey |
| **Fox** | earth, lair | | **Tiger** | lair |
| **Hare** | form | | **Wasp** | nest, vespiary |

# TOP TEN WORLD'S LARGEST SPIDERS (AVERAGE LEG SPAN)

| 1 | Huntsman spider | 300 mm |
|---|---|---|
| 2 | Brazilian salmon pink tarantula | 270 mm |
| 3 | Brazilian giant tawny red tarantula | 260 mm |
| =4 | Goliath tarantula | 254 mm |
| =4 | Wolf spider | 254 mm |
| =6 | Purple bloom bird-eating spider | 230 mm |
| =6 | Colombian lesser black tarantula | 230 mm |
| 8 | Hercules baboon spider | 203 mm |
| 9 | Cameroon red baboon spider | 178 mm |
| 10 | Cardinal spider | 140 mm |

# MAJOR EXTINCTIONS IN THE LAST 2,000 YEARS

| MAMMAL | HABITAT | EXTINCTION |
|---|---|---|
| European lion | Greece | 100 |
| European ass (equus) | Spain | 1400 |
| Auroch | Poland | 1610 |
| Corsican pika | Corsica, France | 1800 |
| Sardinian pika | Sardinia, Italy | 1800 |
| Tarpan | Poland | 1800 |
| Caucasian moose | Caucasus Mountains | 1810 |
| Portugese ibex | Portugal | 1892 |
| Caucasian wisent | Caucasus Mountains | 1927 |
| Caspian tiger | South-west Russia | 1960s |
| Majorcan hare | Majorca, Spain | 1980 |
| Cyprus spiny mouse | Cyprus | 1980 |
| Pyrenean ibex | Spain | 2000 |
| West African black rhino | Cameroon | 2011 |

| BIRD | HABITAT | EXTINCTION |
|---|---|---|
| Dodo | Mauritius | 1600s |
| Great auk | Iceland | 1844 |
| Cyprus dipper | Cyprus | 1950 |
| Alaotra grebe | Madagascar | 2010 |

| REPTILE | HABITAT | EXTINCTION |
|---|---|---|
| Ratas Island lizard | Menorca, Spain | 1950 |
| Santo Stefano lizard | Santo Stefano Island, Italy | 1965 |
| Golden toad | Costa Rica | 2004 |

# TOP TEN WORLD'S MOST VENOMOUS ANIMALS

| 1 | **Box jellyfish** |
|----|----|
| 2 | King cobra |
| 3 | Cone snail |
| 4 | Blue-ringed octopus |
| 5 | Deathstalker scorpion |
| 6 | Stonefish |
| 7 | Brazilian wandering spider |
| 8 | Inland taipan |
| 9 | Poison dart frog |
| 10 | Pufferfish |

## Fascinating Facts

- There have been 5,568 recorded deaths worldwide caused by box jellyfish since 1954. They have up to 60 tentacles and each one contains enough toxins to kill 50 people.

- The inland taipan carries enough venom to kill 100 people but there are no recorded fatalities.

**TOP TEN ENDANGERED SPECIES IN 2016**

| 1 | Javan rhinoceros | Fewer than 60 |
|---|---|---|
| 2 | Amur leopard | 70 |
| 3 | Vaquita | Fewer than 100 |
| 4 | Mountain gorilla | 880 |
| 5 | Yangtze finless porpoise | 1,000–1,080 |
| 6 | Giant panda | 1,864 |
| 7 | Sumatran elephant | 2,400–2,800 |
| 8 | Tiger | 3,890 |
| 9 | Snow leopard | 4,000–6,500 |
| 10 | Sumatran orangutan | 7,300 |

Giraffes are facing a silent extinction with only 90,000 left in the wild in 2016, compared to 150,000 in 2001.

 **TOP TEN WORLD'S BIGGEST DINOSAURS**

| 1 | Argentinosaurus | 100 t / 36.58 m (120 ft) |
|---|---|---|
| 2 | Sauroposeidon | over 60 t / 29.87 m (98 ft) |
| 3 | Spinosaurus | 13 t / 15.85 m (52 ft) |
| 4 | Shantungosaurus | 50 t / 15.24 m (50 ft) |
| =5 | Liopleurodon | 30 t / 15.24 m (50 ft) |
| =5 | Shonisaurus | 30 t / 15.24 m (50 ft) |
| 7 | Quetzalcoatlus | 100 kg / 13.72 m (45 ft) |
| 8 | Sarcosuchus | 8 t / 12.19 m (40 ft) |
| 9 | Utahraptor | 0.68 t / 6.10 m (20 ft) |
| 10 | Moschops | 1 t / 4.88 m (16 ft) |

## Fascinating Facts

- The first fossil ever investigated was the femur of a megalosaurus found in 1676 in England. When the fragment was discovered, one Oxford professor concluded that it belonged to a giant human!

- The fossilised remains of an archaeopteryx were discovered in 1860–62 in Solnhofen, Germany. They were found not long after Charles Darwin's *On the Origin of Species* was first published, and this fossil offered support for an evolutionary link between dinosaurs and birds.

 # TOP TEN WORLD'S SMALLEST ANIMALS

| 1 | Fairy fly | 0.24 mm |
|---|---|---|
| =2 | Anglerfish | 7.9 mm |
| =2 | Paedocypris fish | 7.9 mm |
| 4 | Brazilian gold frog | 9.8 mm |
| 5 | Jaragua sphaero or dwarf gecko lizard | 15.24 mm |
| 6 | Seahorse | 16 mm |
| 7 | Hamster | 22.86 mm |
| 8 | Dwarf chameleon | 38.1 mm |
| 9 | Bee hummingbird | 57.15 mm |
| 10 | Thread snake | 100 mm |

# TOP TEN WORLD'S BIGGEST FISH (RANKED BY LENGTH)

| 1 | Whale shark | 12.65 m (41.5 ft) |
|---|---|---|
| 2 | Basking shark | 12.27 m (40.3 ft) |
| 3 | Beluga or European sturgeon | 8.6 m (28.2 ft) |
| 4 | Great white shark | 6 m (19.7 ft) |
| 5 | Giant freshwater stingray | 5.03 m (16.5 ft) |
| 6 | Bull shark | 4 m (13.1 ft) |
| 7 | Ocean sunfish | 3.2 m (10.5 ft) |
| 8 | Pirarucu | 3 m (9.8 ft) |
| 9 | Wels catfish | 3 m (9.8 ft) |
| 10 | Mekong giant catfish | 2.7 m (8.9 ft) |

# TOP TEN WORLD'S SMELLIEST ANIMALS

| | |
|---|---|
| 1 | **Zorilla** |
| 2 | Skunk |
| 3 | Porcupine |
| 4 | Tasmanian devil |
| 5 | Ferret |
| 6 | Turkey vulture |
| 7 | Kakapo |
| 8 | Mink frog |
| 9 | Stinkpot turtle |
| 10 | Darkling beetle |

## Fascinating Facts

- The zorilla, or striped polecat, lives in arid regions of southern Africa. Its smell is so potent that it can tickle your nostril hairs from half a mile away!

- Herrings communicate through farting. And they fart all the time, which means they must have a lot to talk about!

- The elusive, sweet-toothed binturong is a member of the civet family and lives in the tropical forests of southern Asia. It's a bizarre animal with a scent that is said to be like buttered popcorn.

- Termites, not cows, are the undisputed fart champions of the world. It is estimated they are responsible for as much as 11 per cent of all global methane emissions – twice as much as cows.

# TOP TEN WORLD'S LONGEST-LIVING ANIMALS

| 1 | Quahog (marine clam) | 200+ years* |
|---|---|---|
| 2 | Giant tortoise | 150 years |
| 3 | Greek tortoise | 110 years |
| 4 | Killer whale | 90 years |
| 5 | European eel | 88 years |
| 6 | Lake sturgeon | 82 years |
| 7 | Sea anemone | 80 years |
| 8 | Elephant | 78 years |
| 9 | Freshwater mussel | 75 years |
| 10 | Whale shark | 70 years |

*A marine clam named Ming, the world's oldest animal, was killed in 2006 at 507 years old by scientists trying to find out how old it was!

# TOP TEN LONGEST GESTATION PERIODS

| 1 | Shark (basking, frilled, spiny dogfish) | 730–1,095 days |
|---|---|---|
| 2 | Black alpine salamander | 730+ days |
| 3 | African elephant | 660 days |
| 4 | Asiatic elephant | 600 days |
| 5 | Baird's beaked whale | 520 days |
| 6 | White rhinoceros | 490 days |
| 7 | Walrus | 480 days |
| 8 | Giraffe | 460 days |
| 9 | Velvet worm | 455 days |
| 10 | Tapir | 400 days |

# ART AND ARTISTS

# NATURAL PIGMENTS

| COLOUR | SOURCE |
| --- | --- |
| Crimson (red) | Insect called *Kermes vermilio* |
| Ultramarine (blue) | Lapis lazuli |
| Indigo (dark purple) | Extract of *Indigofera* plant, or the woad or glastum plant |
| Tyrian purple (reddy purple) | Secretions of the sea snail |
| Cochineal (red) | The cochineal insect |
| Burnt sienna (brown) | Iron oxide |
| Verdigris (green) | Copper and vinegar mix |

# THE FIVE MAJOR ORDERS OF CLASSICAL ARCHITECTURE

| | ORDER | FEATURES |
| --- | --- | --- |
| 1 | Doric | Fluted shafts; three vertical bands and square panels |
| 2 | Ionic | Densely fluted shafts, scrolls carved on capital |
| 3 | Corinthian | Fluted column and capital, carved with two rows of acanthus leaves and scrolls |
| 4 | Tuscan | Roman adaptation of Doric; plain shaft, no fluting |
| 5 | Composite | Roman blend of Ionic scrolls and Corinthian acanthus leaves |

# TOP FIVE WORLD'S MOST PROLIFIC ARTISTS

| | |
|---|---|
| 1 | **Morris Katz (1932–2010) – over 280,000 works** |
| 2 | Pablo Picasso (1881–1973) – 147,800 works |
| 3 | Ik-Joong Kang (1960–present) – 40,000 paintings |
| 4 | Pierre-Auguste Renoir (1841–1919) – 6,000 paintings |
| 5 | Bahruz Kangarli (1892–1922) – nearly 4,000 works |

# TOP TEN WORLD'S MOST EXPENSIVE PAINTINGS EVER SOLD

| | |
|---|---|
| 1 | *Les Femmes d'Alger*, **Pablo Picasso: $179.3 million (Christie's, 2015)** |
| 2 | *Number 5, 1948*, Jackson Pollock: $140 million (private sale, 2006) |
| 3 | *Woman III*, Willem de Kooning: $137.5 million (private sale, 2006) |
| 4 | *Portrait of Adele Bloch-Bauer I*, Gustav Klimt: $135 million (private sale, 2006) |
| 5 | *Nu au Plateau de Sculpteur*, Pablo Picasso: $106.5 million (Christie's, 2010) |
| 6 | *Garçon à la Pipe*, Pablo Picasso: $104.1 million (Sotheby's, 2004) |
| 7 | *Eight Elvises*, Andy Warhol: $100 million (private sale, 2008) |
| 8 | *Dora Maar au Chat*, Pablo Picasso: $95.2 million (Sotheby's, 2006) |
| 9 | *Triptych, 1976*, Francis Bacon: $86.3 million (Sotheby's, 2008) |
| 10 | *Portrait of Doctor Gachet*, Vincent van Gogh: $82.5 million (Christie's, 1990) |

# MOST VALUABLE ART THEFTS

| 1 | **Isabella Stewart Gardner Museum, Boston, 1990 – 13 paintings: over $500 million** |
|---|---|
| 2 | Van Gogh Museum, Amsterdam, 1991 – 20 paintings: $500 million |
| 3 | E. G. Bührle Collection, Zurich, 2008 – four major works: $163 million |
| 4 | The Stockholm Modern Museum, Sweden, 1993 – eight works by Picasso and Braque: $60 million |
| 5 | The Stockholm National Museum, Sweden, 2000 – Renoir and Rembrandt paintings: $30 million |
| 6 | National Gallery, London, 1961 – *Portrait of the Duke of Wellington* by Goya: $400,000* |

\* Value at the time of the robbery – worth approximately $3.2 million in 2016

## Fascinating Facts

- When three ski-masked men snatched a Cézanne, a Degas, a van Gogh and a Monet, together worth an estimated $163 million, from a Zurich museum, they failed to take the most expensive paintings in the collection.

- Benvenuto Cellini's *Saliera*, known as 'the *Mona Lisa* of sculpture' and worth $60 million, was stolen from a museum in Vienna in 2003 and spent two years under the bed of the first-time thief before any attempt was made to ransom it; the piece was recovered, and the thief caught, in 2006.

- While revellers partied during the 2006 Rio de Janeiro carnival, four armed men used the chaos to make off with paintings worth at least $20 million from a nearby museum.

- Goya's famous painting of the Duke of Wellington was snatched from London's National Gallery in 1961 only to reappear in the lair of Doctor No during the first James Bond film. The real painting was returned voluntarily six years later.

# TOP TEN WORLD'S MOST FAKED ARTISTS

| | |
|---|---|
| **1** | **Giorgio de Chirico (1888–1978)** |
| 2 | Jean-Baptiste-Camille Corot (1796–1875) |
| 3 | Salvador Dalí (1904–89) |
| 4 | Honoré Daumier (1808–79) |
| 5 | Vincent van Gogh (1853–90) |
| 6 | Kazimir Malevich (1878–1935) |
| 7 | Amedeo Modigliani (1884–1920) |
| 8 | Frederic Remington (1861–1909) |
| 9 | Auguste Rodin (1840–1917) |
| 10 | Maurice Utrillo (1883–1955) |

 # TOP TEN WORLD'S BIGGEST ARTWORKS

| | |
|---|---|
| **1** | ***Mundi Man* or *Eldee Man*, Ando: 4 million sq m (43.06 million sq ft)** |
| 2 | *Surrounded Islands*, Christo and Jeanne-Claude: 603,850 sq m (6.5 million sq feet) |
| 3 | *The Wave*, Djuro Siroglavic: 13,000 sq m (139,932 sq ft) |
| 4 | *Mother Earth*, David Aberg: 7,989 sq m (86,000 sq ft) |
| 5 | *Smiley Face*, Students of Robb College, New South Wales: 6,729 sq m (72,437 sq ft) |
| 6 | *Hero*, Eric Waugh: 3,846 sq m (41,400 sq ft) |
| 7 | *Battle of Borodino*, Franz Roubaud: 1,725 sq m (18,567 sq ft) |
| 8 | *The Big Picture*, Ando: 1,200 sq m (12,916 sq ft) |
| 9 | *Panorama Mesdag*, Hendrik Willem Mesdag: 1,145.9 sq m (12,334 sq ft) |
| 10 | *The Battle of Atlanta*, American Panorama Company: 947.43 sq m (10,198 sq ft) |

# TURNER PRIZE WINNERS (2006–2015)

| YEAR | ARTIST |
| --- | --- |
| 2006 | Tomma Abts |
| 2007 | Mark Wallinger |
| 2008 | Mark Leckey |
| 2009 | Richard Wright |
| 2010 | Susan Philipsz |
| 2011 | Martin Boyce |
| 2012 | Elizabeth Price |
| 2013 | Laure Prouvost |
| 2014 | Duncan Campbell |
| 2015 | Assemble |

# TOP FIVE MOST EXPENSIVE SCULPTURES SOLD AT AUCTION

| 1 | *L'Homme au Doigt (Pointing Man)*, **Alberto Giacometti**. Sold at Christie's, New York, May 2015, for $141.3 million |
|---|---|
| 2 | *L'Homme Qui Marche I*, **Alberto Giacometti**. Sold at Sotheby's, London, February 2010, for $104.3 million |
| 3 | *Chariot*, **Alberto Giacometti**. Sold at Sotheby's, New York, November 2014, for $101 million |
| 4 | *Tête*, **Amedeo Modigliani**. Sold at Christie's, Paris, June 2010, for $59.5 million |
| 5 | *Balloon Dog (Orange)*, **Jeff Koons**. Sold at Christie's, New York, November 2013, for $58.4 million |

# TOP TEN WORLD'S OLDEST ARTWORKS

| =1 | **Auditorium Cave petroglyphs (rock carvings), Madhya Pradesh, central India: 290,000–700,000 BC** |
|---|---|
| =1 | **Daraki-Chattan Cave petroglyphs (rock carvings), Madhya Pradesh, central India: 290,000–700,000 BC** |
| 3 | *Venus of Berekhat Ram* (basaltic figurine), Golan Heights, Israel: 230,000–700,000 BC |
| 4 | *Venus of Tan-Tan* (quartzite figurine), Tan-Tan, Morocco: 200,000–500,000 BC |
| 5 | Blombos Cave rock art, South Africa: 70,000 BC |
| 6 | La Ferrassie Cave cupules (cupules on a Neanderthal tomb), Les Eyzies, Dordogne, France: 70,000–40,000 BC |
| 7 | Swabian Jura ivory carvings, Germany: 33,000–30,000 BC |
| =8 | Bone *Venus of Kostenki*, Russia: 30,000 BC |
| =8 | *Venus of Monpazier* (steatite statuette), France: 30,000 BC |
| 10 | Chauvet Cave paintings, Ardèche, France: 30,000–23,000 BC |

## Fascinating Facts

- Visitors to the State Hermitage Museum in St Petersburg, Russia, have to walk 15 miles to see the 322 galleries, housing nearly three million works of art.

- As an engineer, Leonardo da Vinci conceived ideas vastly ahead of his own time, conceptually inventing a helicopter, a tank, the use of concentrated solar power, a calculator, a rudimentary theory of plate tectonics, the double hull and many others.

- In 1961, Matisse's *Le Bateau* (*The Boat*) hung upside down for two months in the Museum of Modern Art, New York (none of the 116,000 visitors had noticed).

- Vincent van Gogh sold only one painting during his lifetime; *The Red Vineyard at Arles* was bought for 400 francs by Anna Boch.

# COMPUTER
# SCIENCE

# KEY DATES IN THE HISTORY OF COMPUTERS

**1833** – Charles Babbage designs the first general purpose 'Analytical Engine'.

**1842** – Ada Augusta King-Noel, Countess of Lovelace, weaves instructions on punched cards, based on a language compatible with the 'Analytical Engine' – she is often regarded as the first computer programmer.

**1941** – Konrad Zuse develops his Z3 computer in Berlin, Germany, which uses the binary number system and performs floating-point arithmetic.

**1946** – Konrad Zuse develops the world's first programming language: Plankalkül.

**1949** – Maurice Wilkes and the staff of the mathematical laboratory at Cambridge University in the UK develop EDSAC, the first fully functional, stored-programme computer.

**1950** – The floppy disk is invented at the Imperial University in Tokyo by Doctor Yoshiro Nakamatsu.

**1976** – The first Apple computer – the Apple 1 – is shown to the public.

**1989** – Tim Berners-Lee invents the World Wide Web.

**1995** – The first online bookstore – Amazon.com – is launched by Jeff Bezos.

**1995** – eBay is founded by Pierre Omidyar.

**1998** – Larry Page and Sergey Bin found Google.

**2004** – Facebook is launched.

**2007** – The Apple iPhone brings many functions of a computer to the smartphone.

**2012** – Apple launches the iPad.

**2016** – Apple releases the iPhone 7.

# TOP TEN FASTEST SUPERCOMPUTERS*

|     | COMPUTER             | MANUFACTURER | LOCATION     |
| --- | -------------------- | ------------ | ------------ |
| 1   | **Sunway TaihuLight** | **NRCPC**    | **China**    |
| 2   | Tianhe-2 (MilkyWay-2) | NUDT         | China        |
| 3   | Titan                | Cray Inc.    | USA          |
| 4   | Sequoia              | IBM          | USA          |
| 5   | K Computer           | Fujitsu      | Japan        |
| 6   | Mira                 | IBM          | USA          |
| 7   | Trinity              | Cray Inc.    | USA          |
| 8   | Piz Daint            | Cray Inc.    | Switzerland  |
| 9   | Hazel Hen            | Cray Inc.    | Germany      |
| 10  | Shaheen II           | Cray Inc.    | Saudi Arabia |

\* As of June 2016

 # UNITS OF DATA

**1 bit** – The smallest unit of data used by a computer

**4 bits** – Nybble (semioctet)

**8 bits** – Byte (octet) (a character of information, e.g. 'a')

**16 bits** – Word (two octets)

**32 bits** – Dword

**64 bits** – Qword

**1 kilobyte** – A thousand characters of information

**1 megabyte** – A million characters of information

**1 gigabyte** – A billion characters of information

**1 terabyte** – A thousand billion characters of information

# TOP TEN WORLD'S BESTSELLING GAME CONSOLES

|  | CONSOLE | YEAR OF RELEASE | UNITS SOLD |
|---|---|---|---|
| 1 | **Sony PlayStation 2** | **2000** | **157.6 million** |
| 2 | Nintendo DS | 2006 | 154 million |
| 3 | Nintendo Game Boy | 1989 | 118.7 million |
| 4 | Sony PlayStation | 1994 | 104.25 million |
| 5 | Nintendo Wii | 2006 | 101.56 million |
| 6 | Microsoft Xbox 360 | 2005 | 84 million |
| 7 | Sony PlayStation 3 | 2006 | 83.8 million |
| 8 | Nintendo Game Boy Advance | 2001 | 81.51 million |
| 9 | Sony PlayStation Portable (PSP) | 2004 | 80 million |
| 10 | Nintendo Entertainment System (NES) | 1983 | 61.91 million |

## Fascinating Facts

- The commercial for the Macintosh – Apple's first Apple Mac computer – was made by *Alien* director Ridley Scott and cost $1.5 million.

- Over 400,000,000 iPods have been sold worldwide.

- Over a billion iPhones have been sold worldwide.

# APPLE PRODUCTS

| PRODUCT | YEAR OF RELEASE | DESCRIPTION |
| --- | --- | --- |
| Apple I | 1976 | Personal computer |
| Apple II | 1977 | Personal computer |
| Apple III | 1980 | Personal computer |
| Lisa | 1983 | Personal computer |
| Macintosh 128K | 1984 | First original Apple Mac |
| Macintosh Portable | 1989 | Apple's first battery-powered portable PC |
| Powerbook | 1991 | Laptop |
| Power Macintosh | 1994 | Workstation PC |
| iMac | 1998 | Desktop PC |
| iBook | 1999 | Laptop |
| iPod | 2001 | Portable media player |
| Mac mini | 2005 | Small desktop computer |
| MacBook | 2006 | Laptop* |
| Apple TV | 2007 | Digital media receiver |
| iPhone | 2007 | Smartphone |
| MacBook Air | 2008 | Ultraportable laptop |
| iPad | 2010 | Tablet computer |
| iCloud | 2011 | Cloud storage and computing service |
| iPad Mini | 2012 | Mini tablet computer |
| Apple Watch | 2015 | Smartwatch |
| iPhone 7 | 2016 | Smartphone |

* The bestselling Macintosh in history

# TOP PAID APPS FOR IPHONE IN 2016*

| 1 | **Minecraft: Pocket Edition** |
|---|---|
| 2 | Heads Up! |
| 3 | Teeny Titans – A Teen Titans Go! |
| 4 | Akinator the Genie |
| 5 | Grand Theft Auto: San Andreas |
| 6 | Facetune |
| 7 | 7 Minute Workout Challenge |
| 8 | Geometry Dash |
| 9 | Bloons TD 5 |
| 10 | The Game of Life: Classic Edition |

\* As of June 2016

 # TOP TEN MOST POPULAR WEBSITES ON THE INTERNET*

| 1 | **Google.com** |
|---|---|
| 2 | Youtube.com |
| 3 | Facebook.com |
| 4 | Baidu.com |
| 5 | Yahoo.com |
| 6 | Amazon.com |
| 7 | Wikipedia.org |
| 8 | qq.com |
| 9 | Google.co.in |
| 10 | Twitter.com |

\* As of June 2016

# TOP FIVE WEB BROWSERS WORLDWIDE WITH MARKET SHARE*

| | |
|---|---|
| 1 | **Chrome – 57.1 per cent** |
| 2 | Safari – 13.8 per cent |
| 3 | Firefox – 10.9 per cent |
| 4 | Internet Explorer and Edge – 10.4 per cent |
| 5 | Opera – 3.1 per cent |

\* As of June 2016

# TOP FIVE MOST POPULAR SEARCH ENGINES IN THE USA*

| | SEARCH ENGINE | ESTIMATED UNIQUE MONTHLY VISITORS |
|---|---|---|
| 1 | **Google** | **1.6 billion** |
| 2 | Bing | 400 million |
| 3 | Yahoo! Search | 300 million |
| 4 | Ask | 245 million |
| 5 | AOL Search | 125 million |

\* As of June 2016

# TOP TEN COUNTRIES WITH HIGHEST NUMBER OF INTERNET USERS*

| | COUNTRY | USERS | PERCENTAGE OF POPULATION |
|---|---|---|---|
| 1 | **China** | **674 million** | **49.5 per cent** |
| 2 | India | 375 million | 30 per cent |
| 3 | USA | 280 million | 87.4 per cent |
| 4 | Brazil | 117 million | 57.6 per cent |
| 5 | Japan | 114 million | 90.6 per cent |
| 6 | Russia | 103 million | 70.5 per cent |
| 7 | Nigeria | 92 million | 51.1 per cent |
| 8 | Indonesia | 78 million | 30.5 per cent |
| 9 | Germany | 71 million | 88.4 per cent |
| 10 | Mexico | 60 million | 49.3 per cent |

\* As of November 2015. The United Kingdom was eleventh, with 59 million users and 91.6 per cent of the population

# TOP TEN WORST COMPUTER VIRUSES

| | |
|---|---|
| 1 | **The Morris Worm (1998) – affected 10 per cent of all computers connected to the Internet** |
| 2 | The Concept Virus (1995) – infected Microsoft Word documents |
| 3 | CIH aka The Chernobyl Virus (1998) – overwrites a chip, paralysing the computer |
| 4 | The Anna Kournikova Worm (2001) – malicious attachment posing as a photo of the tennis player |
| 5 | ILOVEYOU aka The Love Bug (2000) – designed to steal Internet access passwords |
| 6 | The Melissa Virus (1999) – mass-mailing macro virus that inserted a *Simpsons* quote into Word documents |
| 7 | The Blaster Worm (2003) – launched a denial-of-service attack against Microsoft's website |
| 8 | Netsky Worm (2004) and Sasser Worm (2004) – over a million computers infected |
| 9 | Solar Sunrise (1998) – took control of over 500 systems belonging to the army, government and private sector in the USA |
| 10 | Code Red Worm (2001) – developed to use the power of all infected computers against the White House website; the estimated damage was $2 billion |

# ENGINEERING AND INVENTIONS

## TOP TEN WORLD'S LONGEST SUSPENSION BRIDGES*

| | BRIDGE | LOCATION | LENGTH |
|---|---|---|---|
| 1 | **Akashi Kaikyo** | **Japan** | **1,991 m (6,532 ft)** |
| 2 | Xihoumen | China | 1,650 m (5,413 ft) |
| 3 | The Great Belt (Storebæltsbroen) | Denmark | 1,624 m (5,328 ft) |
| 4 | Yi Sun-sin | South Korea | 1,545m (5,068 ft) |
| 5 | Runyang | China | 1,490 m (4.888 ft) |
| 6 | Fourth Nanjing Yangtze | China | 1,418 m (4.652 ft) |
| 7 | Humber | England | 1,410 m (4,626 ft) |
| 8 | Jiangyin | China | 1,385 m (4,543 ft) |
| 9 | Tsing Ma | China | 1,377 m (4,518 ft) |
| 10 | Hardanger | Norway | 1,310 m (4,297 ft) |

* Length of central span

## TOP TEN WORLD'S LONGEST TUNNELS

| | TUNNEL | LOCATION | LENGTH |
|---|---|---|---|
| 1 | **Gotthard Base** | **Switzerland** | **35.4 miles (57 km)** |
| 2 | Seikan | Japan | 33.5 miles (53.9 km) |
| 3 | Channel | UK/France | 31.3 miles (50.4 km) |
| 4 | Lötschberg Base | Switzerland | 21.5 miles (34.6 km) |
| 5 | Iwate-Ichinohe | Japan | 16 miles (25.7 km) |
| 6 | Lærdal | Norway | 15.2 miles (24.5 km) |
| 7 | Daishimizu | Japan | 13.8 miles (22.2 km) |
| 8 | Wushaoling | China | 13.1 miles (21.1 km) |
| 9 | Simplon | Switzerland/Italy | 12.3 miles (19.8 km) |
| 10 | Vereina | Switzerland | 11.8 miles (19 km) |

# TOP TEN WORLD'S TALLEST BUILDINGS*

| | BUILDING | LOCATION | HEIGHT |
|---|---|---|---|
| 1 | **Burj Khalifa** | **Dubai, United Arab Emirates** | **829 m (2,722 ft) 163 floors** |
| 2 | Makkah Royal Clock Tower Hotel | Mecca, Saudi Arabia | 601 m (1,972 ft) 120 floors |
| 3 | One World Trade Center | New York, USA | 541 m (1,776 ft) 94 floors |
| 4 | Taipei 101 | Taipei, Taiwan | 508 m (1,670 ft) 101 floors |
| 5 | Shanghai World Financial Centre | Shanghai, China | 492 m (1,614 ft) 101 floors |
| 6 | International Commerce Centre | West Kowloon, Hong Kong | 484 m (1,588 ft) 108 floors |
| 7 | Petronas Tower I and II (twin towers) | Kuala Lumpur, Malaysia | 452 m (1,483 ft) 88 floors |
| 8 | Zifeng Tower | Nanjing, China | 450 m (1,480 ft) 66 floors |
| 9 | Willis Tower | Chicago, USA | 442 m (1,450 ft) 110 floors |
| 10 | Jin Mao Building | Shanghai, China | 421 m (1,381 ft) 88 floors |

* Ranking by highest architectural structural element, i.e. spires, statues, etc., not antennae or flagpoles. For example, the Malaysian Petronas Towers (with spire on top) is ranked higher than the USA's Willis Tower (with antenna on top) despite having lower roof and lower highest point (of spire/antenna)

# TOP TEN WORLD'S LONGEST VEHICULAR BRIDGES

| | BRIDGE | TYPE | LOCATION | LENGTH |
|---|---|---|---|---|
| 1 | **Danyang–Kunshan Grand** | **Rail** | **China** | **102.4 miles (164.8 km)** |
| 2 | Changhua–Kaohsiung | Rail | Taiwan | 97.8 miles (157.4 km) |
| 3 | Tianjin Grand | Rail | China | 70.6 miles (113.6 km) |
| 4 | Weinan Weihe Grand | Rail | China | 49.5 miles (79.7 km) |
| 5 | Bang Na | Highway | Thailand | 33.5 miles (54 km) |
| 6 | Beijing Grand | Rail | China | 29.9 miles (48.1 km) |
| 7 | Lake Pontchartrain | Highway | Louisiana, USA | 23.9 miles (38.5 km) |
| 8 | Manchac Swamp | Highway | Louisiana, USA | 22.8 miles (36.7 km) |
| 9 | Yangcun | Rail | China | 22.3 miles (35.9 km) |
| 10 | Hangzhou Bay | Highway | China | 22.2 miles (35.7 km) |

# TOP TEN WORLD'S HIGHEST DAMS

| | DAM | LOCATION | HEIGHT |
|---|---|---|---|
| 1 | **Jinping-1** | **China** | **305 m (1,001 ft)** |
| 2 | Nurek | Tajikistan | 300 m (984 ft) |
| 3 | Xiaowan | China | 292 m (958 ft) |
| 4 | Xiluodu | China | 285.5 m (937 ft) |
| 5 | Grande Dixence | Switzerland | 285 m (935 ft) |
| 6 | Inguri | Georgia | 272 m (892 ft) |
| 7 | Vajont | Italy | 262 m (859 ft) (disused) |
| 8 | Nuozhadu | China | 261.5 m (858 ft) |
| 9 | Chicoasén | Mexico | 261 m (856 ft) |
| 10 | Tehri | India | 260.5 m (855 ft) |

## Fascinating Facts

- One of the oldest man-made structures still standing is the Step Pyramid at Saqqara in Egypt. Built as a tomb for Pharaoh Djoser, it is believed to have been constructed between 2667 and 2648 BC.

- The Neolithic temple of Ħaġar Qim, located on the Mediterranean island of Malta, is thought to date back to the Ġgantija phase in 3600–3200 BC.

- The oldest known collective human settlement with buildings is Çatalhöyük and dates back to around 7500 BC.

- A structure thought to be the world's oldest building – twice the age of the pyramids – has been found beneath the sea off the coast of Japan and consists of a rectangular stone ziggurat believed to have been built in 8000 BC.

# TOP TEN LONGEST BRITISH RAIL TUNNELS

| | TUNNEL | LOCATION | LENGTH |
|---|---|---|---|
| **1** | **Severn** | **Bristol to Newport** | **4.28 miles (6.88 km)** |
| 2 | Totley | Manchester to Sheffield | 3.44 miles (5.70 km) |
| 3 | Standedge | Manchester to Huddersfield | 3.04 miles (4.89 km) |
| 4 | Sodbury | Swindon to Bristol | 2.53 miles (4.06 km) |
| 5 | Strood | Medway, Kent | 2.24 miles (3.61 km) |
| 6 | Disley | Stockport to Sheffield | 2.2 miles (3.54 km) |
| =7 | Ffestiniog | Llandudno to Blaenau Ffestiniog | 2.14 miles (3.44 km) |
| =7 | Bramhope | Horsforth to Weeton | 2.14 miles (3.44 km) |
| 9 | Cowburn | Manchester to Sheffield | 2.1 miles (3.39 km) |
| 10 | North Downs | Maidstone, Kent | 1.99 miles (3.2 km) |

## Fascinating Facts

- There are some 10,460 miles (16,833 km) of railway in the UK.

- The longest station platform in the UK is at Gloucester station and is 602.6 m (1,977 ft) long.

- Network Rail has 40,000 bridges, tunnels and viaducts throughout Great Britain, as well as around 9,000 level crossings and over 1,100 signal boxes.

# MOST TOXIC MAN-MADE CHEMICALS*

Dioxin

Aldrin

Chlordane

Dichlorodiphenyltrichloroethane (DDT)

Dieldrin

Endrin

Heptachlor

Mirex

Toxaphene

Polychlorinated biphenyl (PCB)

Hexachlorobenzene

Furan

* These chemicals are on a list produced for the 2001 Stockholm Convention on Persistent Organic Pollutants (POPs)

# TOP FIVE WORLD'S DEEPEST MINES

| | MINE | LOCATION | DEPTH |
|---|---|---|---|
| 1 | **Mponeng** | **Johannesburg, South Africa** | **over 2.5 miles (4 km)** |
| 2 | Savuka | West Wits, South Africa | 2.3 miles (3.7 km) |
| 3 | Driefontein | Carletonville, South Africa | 2.1 miles (3.4 km) |
| 4 | Kusasalethu | Carletonville, South Africa | 2 miles (3.27 km) |
| 5 | Moab Khotsong | Johannesburg, South Africa | 1.9 miles (3.05 km) |

# TOP TEN WORLD'S BIGGEST POWER STATIONS BY OUTPUT

| 1 | **Three Gorges Dam (hydroelectric)** | **China** | **22,500 MW** |
|---|---|---|---|
| 2 | Itaipu Dam (hydroelectric) | Brazil/Paraguay | 14,000 MW |
| 3 | Xiluodu Dam (hydroelectric) | China | 13,860 MW |
| 4 | Guri Dam (hydroelectric) | Venezuela | 10,235 MW |
| 5 | Tucuruí Dam (hydroelectric) | Brazil | 8,370 MW |
| 6 | Kashiwazaki-Kariwa Nuclear Power Plant | Japan | 7,965 MW |
| 7 | Grand Coulee Dam (hydroelectric) | USA | 6,809 MW |
| 8 | Xiangjiaba Dam (hydroelectric) | China | 6,448 MW |
| 9 | Longtan Dam (hydroelectric) | China | 6,426 MW |
| 10 | Sayano–Shushenskaya Dam (hydroelectric) | Russia | 6,400 MW |

# TOP TEN WORLD'S LARGEST DIAMONDS

| 1 | Golden Jubilee | 545.67 ct |
|---|---|---|
| 2 | Star of Africa | 530.20 ct |
| 3 | The Incomparable | 407.48 ct |
| 4 | The Cullinan II | 317.40 ct |
| 5 | Spirit of de Grisogono | 312.24 ct |
| 6 | Centenary | 273.83 ct |
| 7 | Jubilee | 245.35 ct |
| 8 | The De Beers | 234.65 ct |
| 9 | The Red Cross | 205.07 ct |
| 10 | Millennium Star | 203.4 ct |

## Fascinating Facts

- The depth of the Mirny diamond mine hole is such that wind currents inside cause a downdraft that has resulted in helicopters being sucked in. It produces 10 million carats of diamond per year.

- The famous Hope diamond is supposedly cursed. Legend has it that the jewel was removed from the eye socket of a Hindu statue in India and has since brought bad luck to its subsequent owners in the form of bankruptcy, insanity, suicide and even being torn apart by wild dogs!

# THE MOHS SCALE*

Talc

Gypsum

Calcite

Fluorite

Apatite

Orthoclase

Quartz

Topaz

Corundum

Diamond

\* Named after German mineralogist Friedrich Mohs, the scale is used for comparing relative hardness of minerals. Each mineral on the scale can be scratched by the harder ones below it

# TOP FIVE WORLD'S LONGEST HIGHWAYS

|   | HIGHWAY | LOCATION | LENGTH |
|---|---------|----------|--------|
| 1 | **Pan-American** | **North Alaska to Argentina** | **30,000 miles (48,280 km)** |
| 2 | Highway 1 | Australia | 15,534 miles (25,000 km) |
| 3 | Trans-Siberian | St Petersburg to Vladivostck, Russia | 6,835 miles (11,000 km) |
| 4 | Trans-Canada | Vancouver Island to St John's, Newfoundland | 4,860 miles (7,821 km) |
| 5 | Golden Quadrilateral | India | 3,633 miles (5,864 km) |

# TOP TEN WORLD'S MOST DANGEROUS ROADS

| 1 | **North Yungas Road aka 'The Road of Death', Bolivia** |
|---|---|
| 2 | Commonwealth Avenue aka 'Killer Highway', Philippines |
| 3 | James Dalton Highway, Alaska |
| 4 | BR-116 aka 'The Highway of Death', Brazil |
| 5 | The Himalayan Roads |
| 6 | Guoliang Tunnel Road, Taihang Mountains, China |
| 7 | Taroko Gorge Road, Taiwan |
| 8 | Strada delle 52 Gallerie (Road of 52 Tunnels), Pasubio, Italy |
| 9 | Halsema Highway, Philippines |
| 10 | Skippers Canyon Road, New Zealand |

## Fascinating Facts

- The North Yungas is believed to be the most dangerous road in the world. It stretches for about 40 mountain-hugging miles and is only 10 feet wide.

- 'Guoliang' translates from Chinese as 'the road that does not tolerate any mistakes'. The tunnel road is 4.5 m high and 3.7 m wide with 30 'windows' to enjoy the dramatic landscape.

# TOP TEN WORLD'S TALLEST CHURCHES

| | CHURCH | LOCATION | HEIGHT |
|---|---|---|---|
| 1 | **Chicago Methodist Temple** | **USA** | **173 m (568 ft)** |
| 2 | Sagrada Familia | Barcelona, Spain* | 170 m (558 ft) |
| 3 | Ulm Cathedral | Ulm, Germany | 162 m (530 ft) |
| 4 | Basilica of Our Lady of Peace, Yamoussoukro | Ivory Coast | 158 m (518 ft) |
| 5 | Cologne Cathedral | Cologne, Germany | 157 m (516 ft) |
| 6 | Rouen Cathedral | Rouen France | 151 m (495 ft) |
| 7 | St Nicholas Church | Hamburg, Germany | 147 m (482 ft) |
| 8 | Notre-Dame Cathedral | Strasbourg, France | 144 m (472 ft) |
| 9 | Basilica of Our Lady of Licheń | Licheń, Poland | 140 m (459 ft) |
| 10 | St Peter's Basilica | Rome, Italy | 138 m (452 ft) |

* To be completed in 2026

# INVENTIONS AND THEIR INVENTORS

| INVENTION | INVENTOR | PLACE | YEAR |
|---|---|---|---|
| 3D printing | Chuck Hull | USA | 1984 |
| Adding machine | Blaise Pascal | France | 1642 |
| Aeroplane | Orville and Wilbur Wright | USA | 1903 |

| INVENTION | INVENTOR | PLACE | YEAR |
|---|---|---|---|
| Ambulance | Dominique-Jean Larrey | France | 1792 |
| Aqualung | Jacques Cousteau and Emile Gagnan | France | 1943 |
| Atomic bomb | Otto Frisch, Niels Bohr, Rudolf Peierls | Austria, Denmark, Germany | 1939–45 |
| Automatic loom | Joseph-Marie Jacquard | France | 1801 |
| Ballpoint pen | Ladislao Biro | Hungary | 1944 |
| Barometer | Evangelista Torricelli | Italy | 1643 |
| Battery (electric) | Alessandro Volta | Italy | 1800 |
| Bicycle (self-propelled) | Kirkpatrick Macmillan | UK | 1839–40 |
| Bouncing bomb | Barnes Wallis | UK | 1943 |
| Car (internal combustion) | Gottlieb Daimler | Germany | 1884 |
| Car (petrol) | Karl Benz | Germany | 1886 |
| Cash register | William Burroughs | USA | 1892 |
| Cat's eyes | Percy Shaw | UK | 1934 |
| Cement (Portland) | Joseph Aspdin | UK | 1824 |
| Cinema | Auguste and Louis Lumière | France | 1895 |
| Clock (mechanical) | Yi Xing | China | AD 725 |
| Coffee (instant) | Nestlé | Switzerland | 1937 |
| Contraceptive pill | Gregor Pincus | USA | 1950 |

| INVENTION | INVENTOR | PLACE | YEAR |
|---|---|---|---|
| Credit card | Ralph Schneider and Frank McNamara | USA | 1950 |
| Crossword | Arthur Wynne | USA | 1913 |
| Diesel engine | Rudolf Diesel | Germany | 1894 |
| Digital camera | Gareth Lloyd and Steven Sasson | USA | 1977 |
| Electric chair | Harold P. Brown and Arthur E. Kennelly | USA | 1888 |
| Electric guitar | Adolph Rickenbacker, Paul Barth and George D. Beauchamp | USA | 1931 |
| Electric light bulb | Thomas Edison | USA | 1879 |
| Electric telegraph | Georges Louis Lesage | Switzerland | 1774 |
| Escalator | Jesse W. Reno | USA | 1892 |
| Film (with soundtrack) | Lee de Forest | USA | 1919 |
| Flying shuttle | John Kay | UK | 1733 |
| Fountain pen | Lewis E. Waterman | USA | 1884 |
| Frozen food processor | Clarence Birdseye | USA | 1929 |
| Helicopter (first-manned) | Louis and Jacques Bréguet | France | 1907 |
| Hovercraft | Christopher Cockerell | UK | 1956 |
| Jeans | Levi-Strauss | USA | 1872 |

| INVENTION | INVENTOR | PLACE | YEAR |
|---|---|---|---|
| Jet engine | Frank Whittle | UK | 1930 |
| Lawnmower | James Edward Ransome | UK | 1902 |
| Light bulb | Joseph Swan / Thomas Edison | UK/USA | 1878 |
| Machine gun | James Puckle | UK | 1718 |
| Margarine | Hippolyte Megé-Mouriès | France | 1868 |
| Match | Robert Boyle | UK | 1680 |
| Mechanical computer | Charles Babbage | UK | 1835 |
| Microscope | Zacharias Janssen | The Netherlands | 1590 |
| Microwave oven | Percy Lebaron Spencer | USA | 1946 |
| Miner's safety lamp | Humphry Davy | UK | 1815 |
| Motorcycle | Gottleib Daimler | Germany | 1885 |
| Nylon | Wallace H. Carothers | USA | 1938 |
| Paper clip | Johan Vaaler | Norway | 1899 |
| Passenger lift / elevator | Elisha Graves Otis | USA | 1857 |
| Pencil | Nicolas-Jacques Conté | France | 1795 |
| Photographic film | George Eastman | USA | 1889 |
| Pianoforte | Bartolomeo Cristofori | Italy | 1720 |
| Plastics | John W. Hyatt | USA | 1868 |
| Pneumatic bicycle tyre | John Boyd Dunlop | UK | 1888 |

**MAN FACTS**

| INVENTION | INVENTOR | PLACE | YEAR |
|---|---|---|---|
| Pocket calculator | Jack Kilby, James Van Tassell and Jerry Merryman | USA | 1972 |
| Power loom | Edmund Cartwright | UK | 1785 |
| Printing press | Johannes Gutenberg | Germany | 1450 |
| Radar | Robert Watson-Watt | UK | 1935 |
| Radio (transatlantic) | Guglielmo Marconi | Italy | 1901 |
| Razor (safety) | King Camp Gillette | USA | 1895 |
| Record (LP) | Peter Goldmark | USA | 1948 |
| Revolver | Samuel Colt | USA | 1835 |
| Safety pin | Walter Hunt | USA | 1849 |
| Scotch tape | Richard Drew | USA | 1930 |
| Sewing machine | Barthélemy Thimonnier | France | 1830 |
| Skyscraper | William Le Baron Jenney | USA | 1882 |
| Spinning Jenny | James Hargreaves | UK | 1764 |
| Spinning mule | Samuel Crompton | UK | 1779 |
| Stapler | Charles Henry Gould | UK | 1868 |
| Steam engine (development) | James Watt | UK | 1765 |
| Steam locomotive | Richard Trevithick | UK | 1804 |
| Steel (stainless) | Harry Brearley | UK | 1913 |
| Stethoscope | René Théophile H. Laënnec | France | 1816 |

| INVENTION | INVENTOR | PLACE | YEAR |
|---|---|---|---|
| Submarine | Cornelius Drebbel | The Netherlands | 1620 |
| Sunscreen | Eugène Schueller | France | 1936 |
| Tank | Ernest Swinton | UK | 1916 |
| Telephone | Alexander Graham Bell | USA | 1876 |
| Telescope (reflecting) | Isaac Newton | UK | 1668 |
| Telescope (refracting) | Hans Lippershey | The Netherlands | 1608 |
| Television | John Logie Baird | UK | 1926 |
| Traffic lights | J. P. Knight | UK | 1868 |
| Typewriter | William Burt | USA | 1829 |
| Vacuum cleaner (electric) | Hubert Cecil Booth | UK | 1901 |
| Vending machine | Percival Everitt | UK | 1883 |
| Washing machine (electric) | Hurley Machine Company | USA | 1908 |
| Water frame | Richard Arkwright | UK | 1769 |
| Zip fastener | Whitcomb L. Judson | USA | 1893 |

**MAN FACTS**

## Fascinating Facts

- American chemist Thomas Midgley, who developed both the environmentally deadly tetraethyl lead additive to petrol and chlorofluorocarbons (CFCs), died of strangulation in 1944 due to another of his inventions. Disabled from polio, he became entangled in the ropes of a system to help him out of bed.

- When British merchant Peter Durand invented the metal can in 1810, he overlooked the need for a device to open it.

- The telescope was accidentally discovered when Hans Lippershey looked through two lenses and saw that the image was magnified.

- The first rickshaw was invented in 1869 by Rev. E. Jonathan Scobie to transport his invalid wife around the streets of Yokohama.

- The Band-Aid was invented by a Johnson & Johnson employee, Earl Dickson. His wife was rather accident-prone so he devised a bandage that she could apply without help.

- The Slinky toy was the result of a failed attempt by engineer Richard James to produce an anti-vibration device for ship instruments. His goal was to develop a metre designed to monitor horsepower on naval battleships. James was working with tension springs when one of the springs fell to the ground. He saw how the spring kept moving after it hit the ground and an idea for a toy was born.

- Kleenex tissue was originally designed to be a gas-mask filter. It was developed at the beginning of World War One to replace cotton, which was then in short supply as a surgical dressing.

- X-ray was discovered purely by accident. When German physicist Wilhelm Conrad Röntgen was experimenting with cathode rays in 1895, he put an activated Crookes tube in a book and went out to lunch. When he returned, he discovered that a key that had also been placed in the book showed up as an image on the developed film.

# FILM

# TOP TEN GREATEST FILMS EVER MADE*

| 1 | *The Shawshank Redemption* (1994) |
| 2 | *The Godfather* (1972) |
| 3 | *The Godfather: Part II* (1974) |
| 4 | *The Dark Knight* (2008) |
| 5 | *Schindler's List* (1993) |
| 6 | *12 Angry Men* (1957) |
| 7 | *Pulp Fiction* (1994) |
| 8 | *The Lord of the Rings: The Return of the King* (2003) |
| 9 | *The Good, the Bad and the Ugly* (1966) |
| 10 | *Fight Club* (1999) |

\* As rated by IMDb (Internet Movie Database) users, June 2016

## Fascinating Fact

- The iconic Hollywood sign is made up of 50 ft-high letters. They stand near the tip of Beachwood Canyon's Mount Lee, the highest peak in Los Angeles. The letters were built in 1923 by property developers to advertise their new sites, called Hollywoodland. It was only in the 1940s, when the film business ballooned, that the last four letters were removed.

# TOP TEN BIGGEST FILM BUDGETS*

| 1 | *Pirates of the Caribbean: On Stranger Tides* | **Walt Disney Studios (2011)** | **$378.5 million** |
|---|---|---|---|
| 2 | *Pirates of the Caribbean: At World's End* | Buena Vista Pictures (2007) | $300 million |
| 3 | *Avengers: Age of Ultron* | Walt Disney Studios (2015) | $279.9 million |
| 4 | *John Carter* | Walt Disney Studios (2012) | $263 million |
| 5 | *Tangled* | Walt Disney Studios (2010) | $260 million |
| 6 | *Spider-Man 3* | Columbia Pictures (2007) | $258 million |
| =7 | *Harry Potter and the Half-Blood Prince* | Warner Bros Pictures (2009) | $250 million |
| =7 | *The Hobbit: The Battle of the Five Armies* | Warner Bros Pictures (2014) | $250 million |
| =7 | *Batman v Superman: Dawn of Justice* | Warner Bros Pictures (2016) | $250 million |
| =7 | *Captain America: Civil War* | Walt Disney Studios (2016) | $250 million |

* Unadjusted for inflation

# TOP TEN HIGHEST-PAID ACTORS (2015 ANNUAL EARNINGS)

| 1 | Robert Downey Jr | $80 million |
|---|---|---|
| 2 | Jennifer Lawrence | $52 million |
| 3 | Jackie Chan | $50 million |
| 4 | Vin Diesel | $47 million |
| 5 | Bradley Cooper | $41.5 million |
| 6 | Adam Sandler | $41 million |
| 7 | Tom Cruise | $40 million |
| 8 | Scarlett Johansson | $35.5 million |
| =9 | Amitabh Bachchan | $33.5 million |
| =9 | Salman Khan | $33.5 million |

# TOP TEN HIGHEST-GROSSING FILMS OF ALL TIME*

| 1 | *Avatar* (2009) | $2.788 billion |
|---|---|---|
| 2 | *Titanic* (1997) | $2.187 billion |
| 3 | *Star Wars: The Force Awakens* (2015) | $2.068 billion |
| 4 | *Jurassic World* (2015) | $1.670 billion |
| 5 | *The Avengers* (2012) | $1.519 billion |
| 6 | *Furious 7* (2015) | $1.516 billion |
| 7 | *Avengers: Age of Ultron* (2015) | $1.405 billion |
| 8 | *Harry Potter and the Deathly Hallows: Part 2* (2011) | $1.341 billion |
| 9 | *Frozen* (2013) | $1.287 billion |
| 10 | *Iron Man 3* (2013) | $1.215 billion |

* As of July 2016 – unadjusted for inflation

# BIGGEST WINNERS AT THE OSCARS IN THE PAST TEN YEARS

| YEAR | CEREMONY | FILM | WINS |
|---|---|---|---|
| 2016 | 88th Academy Awards | *Mad Max: Fury Road* | 6 |
| 2015 | 87th Academy Awards | *Birdman or (The Unexpected Virtue of Ignorance)* and *The Grand Budapest Hotel* | 4 |
| 2014 | 86th Academy Awards | *Gravity* | 7 |
| 2013 | 85th Academy Awards | *The Life of Pi* | 4 |
| 2012 | 84th Academy Awards | *The Artist* and *Hugo* | 5 |
| 2011 | 83th Academy Awards | *Inception* and *The King's Speech* | 4 |
| 2010 | 82nd Academy Awards | *The Hurt Locker* | 6 |
| 2009 | 81st Academy Awards | *Slumdog Millionaire* | 8 |
| 2008 | 80th Academy Awards | *No Country for Old Men* | 4 |
| 2007 | 79th Academy Awards | *The Departed* | 4 |

# ACADEMY AWARD FOR BEST ACTOR IN NUMBERS

**3** – The number of awards Daniel Day-Lewis has won, making him the actor with the most wins in this category.

**8** – The number of nominations Peter O'Toole has received, making him the actor with most nominations without ever having won.

**9** – The age of the youngest nominee, Jackie Cooper, for the film *Skippy*.

**9** – The number of nominations received by both Spencer Tracy and Laurence Olivier, making them the most nominated in the category.

**29** – The age of the youngest winner, Adrian Brody, for the film *The Pianist*.

**76** – The age of the oldest winner, Henry Fonda, for the film *On Golden Pond*.

**79** – The age of the oldest nominee, Richard Farnsworth, for the film *The Straight Story*.

# ACADEMY AWARD FOR BEST ACTRESS IN NUMBERS

**4** – The number of awards Katherine Hepburn has won, making her the actress with the most wins in this category.

**6** – The number of nominations Deborah Kerr has received, making her the actress with the most nominations without ever having won.

**9** – The age of the youngest nominee, Quvenzhané Wallis, for the film *Beasts of the Southern Wild*.

**13** – The number of nominations Meryl Streep has received, making her the actress with the most nominations in the category. (She has won twice.)

**21** – The age of the youngest winner, Marlee Matlin, for the film *Children of a Lesser God*.

**80** – The age of the oldest winner, Jessica Tandy, for the film *Driving Miss Daisy*.

**85** – The age of the oldest nominee, Emmanuelle Riva, for the film *Amour*.

**TOP TEN MOVIE VILLAINS**

| | |
|---|---|
| 1 | **Lord Voldemort, *Harry Potter* series (2005–2011) – played by Ralph Fiennes** |
| 2 | Darth Vader, *Star Wars* series (1977–2005) – played by James Earl Jones, Hayden Christensen |
| 3 | Hannibal Lecter, *Silence of the Lambs* (1991) – played by Anthony Hopkins |
| 4 | The Joker, *The Dark Knight* (2008) – played by Heath Ledger |
| 5 | The Wicked Witch of the West, *The Wizard of Oz* (1939) – played by Margaret Hamilton |
| 6 | Cruella de Vil, *101 Dalmatians* (1961) |
| 7 | Annie Wilkes, *Misery* (1990) – played by Kathy Bates |
| 8 | Freddy Krueger, *A Nightmare on Elm Street* (1984) – played by Robert Englund |
| 9 | The Queen, *Snow White and the Seven Dwarfs* (1937) |
| 10 | Frank Booth, *Blue Velvet* (1986) – played by Dennis Hopper |

# TOP TEN SILVER-SCREEN SUPERHEROES

| | |
|---|---|
| **1** | **Superman (Clark Kent) – played by Christopher Reeve, Brandon Routh and Henry Cavill** |
| 2 | Batman (Bruce Wayne) – played by Adam West, Michael Keaton, Val Kilmer, George Clooney, Christian Bale and Ben Affleck |
| 3 | Spider-Man (Peter Parker) – played by Toby Maguire, Andrew Garfield and Tom Holland |
| 4 | Incredible Hulk (Bruce Banner) – played by Eric Bana and Edward Norton |
| 5 | Wolverine (Logan, from the *X-Men* series) – played by Hugh Jackman |
| 6 | Iron Man (Tony Stark) – played by Robert Downey Jr |
| 7 | Daredevil (Matt Murdock) – played by Ben Affleck |
| 8 | Green Lantern (Hal Jordan) – played by Ryan Reynolds |
| 9 | Elektra (Elektra Natchios) – played by Jennifer Garner |
| 10 | Hellboy (Anung Un Rama) – played by Ron Perlman |

# TOP TEN MOST QUOTED FILM LINES OF ALL TIME

| | LINE | FILM |
|---|---|---|
| 1 | **'I'll be back'** | **_The Terminator_** |
| 2 | 'Frankly, my dear, I don't give a damn' | _Gone with the Wind_ |
| 3 | 'Beam me up, Scotty'* | _Star Trek_ |
| 4 | 'May the force be with you' | _Star Wars_ |
| 5 | 'Life is like a box of chocolates' | _Forrest Gump_ |
| 6 | 'You talking to me?' | _Taxi Driver_ |
| 7 | 'Show me the money' | _Jerry Maguire_ |
| 8 | 'Do you feel lucky, punk?'* | _Dirty Harry_ |
| 9 | 'Here's looking at you, kid' | _Casablanca_ |
| 10 | 'Nobody puts Baby in the corner' | _Dirty Dancing_ |

* Not strictly a verbatim quote

# TOP THREE LONGEST KISSES ON FILM

| | |
|---|---|
| 1 | **Stephanie Sherrin and Gregory Smith in _Kids in America_ (2005): 5 minutes, 57 seconds** |
| 2 | Tina Fey and Steve Carell in _Date Night_ (2010): 4 minutes, 23 seconds |
| 3 | Traci Dinwiddie and Necar Zadegan in _Elena Undone_ (2010): 3 minutes, 24 seconds |

# JAMES BOND FILMS IN ORDER OF NUMBER OF LEAD ACTOR APPEARANCES

| ACTOR | FILMS | YEAR(S) |
| --- | --- | --- |
| Roger Moore | 7 – *Live and Let Die, The Man with the Golden Gun, The Spy Who Loved Me, Moonraker, For Your Eyes Only, Octopussy, A View to a Kill* | (1973) (1974) (1977) (1979) (1981) (1983) (1985) |
| Sean Connery | 6 – *Dr No, From Russia with Love, Goldfinger, Thunderball, You Only Live Twice, Diamonds are Forever* | (1962) (1963) (1964) (1965) (1967) (1971) |
| Pierce Brosnan | 4 – *Goldeneye, Tomorrow Never Dies, The World Is Not Enough, Die Another Day* | (1995) (1997) (1999) (2002) |
| Daniel Craig | 4 – *Casino Royale, Quantum of Solace, Skyfall, Spectre* | (2006) (2008) (2012) (2015) |
| Timothy Dalton | 2 – *The Living Daylights, Licence to Kill* | (1987) (1989) |
| George Lazenby | 1 – *On Her Majesty's Secret Service* | (1969) |

TOP TEN ALFRED HITCHCOCK CAMEOS

1  *The 39 Steps* (1935) – **as Robert Donat and Lucie Mannheim escape the theatre, he can be seen throwing away some rubbish.**

2  *Rope* (1948) – his silhouette is seen on a neon sign.

3  *Dial M for Murder* (1954) – in a photograph in Grace Kelly's apartment (as part of a class reunion picture).

4  *The Man Who Knew Too Much* (1956) – facing away from the camera, watching acrobats in the Moroccan marketplace.

5  *Vertigo* (1958) – walking along a street.

6  *North by Northwest* (1959) – at the end of the opening credits, he just misses his bus.

7  *Psycho* (1960) – as Janet Leigh returns to her office, he is seen through the window, wearing a cowboy hat.

8  *The Birds* (1963) – walking out of a pet shop with two white dogs (they were actually his dogs).

9  *Torn Curtain* (1966) – sitting in a hotel lobby holding a baby.

10  *Topaz* (1969) – being pushed in a wheelchair in an airport, until he gets up, shakes a man's hand and walks away!

# FILMS IN NUMBERS

**24** – The number of times that Arthur Conan Doyle's *The Hound of the Baskervilles* has been adapted for the screen.

**127** – The number of retakes that Shelley Duvall had to do for a single scene in *The Shining*. It holds the world record.

**649** – The number of times, it is thought, that the character Dracula is mentioned in all films. He is also the most depicted character in screen history, making an appearance in over 200 films.

**1958** – The year that Indian comic actress Manorama began her career. In 1985, she appeared in her thousandth movie, making her the most prolific lead performer in film history.

**1,969** – The number of movies produced in India in 2014, and six times the number produced in Hollywood that year.

**5,813** – The number of cinemas in China, meaning that there are 250,000 people to every cinema.

**40,000** – The number of cinemas is the USA, making it the country with the most in the world.

**166,352** – The number of paintings used to create the Disney classic *Snow White and the Seven Dwarfs* (1937).

**615,384** – The cost in dollars per second of the most expensive reel of film in history. The 26-second clip was shot by Abraham Zapruder, and shows the assassination of President Kennedy on 22 November 1963. Its total value is $16 million.

# FOOD AND DRINK

# TOP TEN WORLD'S MOST EXPENSIVE FOODS

| | FOOD | PRICE |
|---|---|---|
| 1 | **1.51 kg Italian white alba truffle** | **$160,406** |
| =2 | 'Frrrozen Haute Chocolate' dessert | $25,000 |
| =2 | 1 kg tin of Almas caviar | $25,000 |
| 4 | Pair of Yubari king melons | $22,872 |
| 5 | 7.7 kg densuke black watermelon | $6,100 |
| 6 | 'FleurBurger 5000' | $5,000 |
| 7 | 12-inch 'Pizza Royale 007' | $4,200 |
| 8 | Samundari Khazana (curry) | $3,200 |
| 9 | Wagyu rib-eye steak | $2,800 |
| 10 | Westin Hotel bagel | $1,000 |

## Fascinating Facts

- The 'Pizza Royale 007' has the most luxurious toppings in the world, including lobster marinated in cognac, caviar soaked in champagne, smoked salmon and 24-carat flakes of edible gold!

- 'Samundari Khazana' means 'seafood treasure' – unsurprising for a curry containing crab, white truffle, caviar, quails' eggs and, you've guessed it, edible gold.

- The $1,000 bagel from New York is topped with white truffle cream and goji berry jelly.

- In the eleventh century, the Church was opposed to the use of forks. So much so that when a Byzantine princess who used a two-pronged gold fork died from the plague, her death was called 'a just punishment from God'.

# WORLD'S BIGGEST SUPERMARKET RETAILERS*

| | SUPERMARKET | COUNTRY | REVENUE IN 2014 | NO. OF STORES |
|---|---|---|---|---|
| 1 | **Walmart** | **USA** | **$485 billion** | **11,453** |
| 2 | Costco | USA | $112 billion | 671 |
| 3 | Kroger | USA | $108 billion | 2,625 |
| 4 | Walgreens Boots Alliance | USA | $103 billion | 12,800 |
| 5 | Tesco | UK | £62.3 billion | 6,814 |
| 6 | Carrefour | France | €74.7 billion | 10,860 |
| 7 | Amazon.com | World's top online retailer | $89 billion | N/A |
| 8 | Metro AG | Germany | €63 billion | 2,200 |
| 9 | The Home Depot, Inc. | USA | $83.2 billon | 2,273 |
| 10 | Target Corporation | USA | $72.6 billion | 1,790 |

* As of 2014

# UK SUPERMARKET'S SHARE OF MARKET*

| 1 | Tesco | 28.2 per cent |
|---|---|---|
| 2 | Sainsbury's | 16.3 per cent |
| 3 | Asda | 15.6 per cent |
| 4 | Morrisons | 10.8 per cent |
| 5 | The Co-operative | 6.3 per cent |
| 6 | Aldi | 6.1 per cent |
| 7 | Waitrose | 5.2 per cent |
| 8 | Lidl | 4.4 per cent |
| 9 | Other outlets | 3.1 per cent |
| 10 | Iceland | 2.1 per cent |

* Calculated over 12 weeks ending 19 June 2016

# TOP FOUR COFFEE CHAINS IN THE UK*

| | CHAIN | NO. OF OUTLETS |
|---|---|---|
| 1 | Costa Coffee | 1,992 |
| 2 | Starbucks | 849 |
| 3 | Caffè Nero | 620 |
| 4 | Tesco | 481 |

* As of 2015

# TOP TEN WORLD'S BIGGEST BEER CONSUMERS

| | COUNTRY | ANNUAL NO. OF PINTS PER PERSON |
|---|---|---|
| **1** | **Czech Republic** | **276.1** |
| 2 | Ireland | 230.7 |
| 3 | Germany | 203.7 |
| 4 | Australia | 193.3 |
| 5 | Austria | 190.5 |
| 6 | Estonia | 183 |
| 7 | UK | 174.2 |
| 8 | Belgium | 163.6 |
| 9 | Romania | 158.3 |
| 10 | Denmark | 158.2 |

# TOP TEN WORLD'S SMELLIEST CHEESES

| | |
|---|---|
| **1** | **Limburger, Germany** |
| 2 | Epoisses de Bourgogne, France |
| 3 | Stinking Bishop, UK |
| 4 | Serra da Estrela, Portugal |
| 5 | Munster d'Alsace, France |
| 6 | Valdeon, Spain |
| 7 | Roquefort, France |
| 8 | Brie de Meaux, France |
| 9 | Camembert de Normandie, France |
| 10 | Pont l'Eveque, France |

# TOP TEN WORLD'S MOST EXPENSIVE BOTTLES OF WINE AND VINTAGE

| | WINE | PRICE |
|---|---|---|
| 1 | **Screaming Eagle Cabernet (1992)** | **£297,000 ($500,000)** |
| 2 | French Cheval-Blanc (1947) | £192,000 ($304,375) |
| 3 | Heidsieck Champagne (1907) | £163,000 ($275,000)* |
| 4 | Château Lafite (1869) | £136,000 ($230,000) |
| 5 | Château Margaux (1787) | £133,000 ($225,000) |
| 6 | Château Lafite (1787) | £92,000 ($156,450) |
| 7 | Château d'Yquem (1811) | £70,000 ($117,000) |
| 8 | Jeroboam of Château Mouton Rothschild (1945) | £67,000 ($114,614) |
| 9 | Château d'Yquem (1787) | £65,000 ($100,000) |
| 10 | Massandra Sherry de la Frontera (1775) | £25,000 ($43,500) |

\* Recovered from shipwreck, after being on the bottom of the sea for over 80 years. The champagne was originally destined for the Imperial Court of Tsar Nicholas II of Russia

## Fascinating Facts

- The most expensive bottle of wine ever, the Screaming Eagle Cabernet, was auctioned in 2000, in Napa Valley, California, for charity and raised $500,000.
- The Château Lafite (1787) and Château d'Yquem (1787) bottles have Thomas Jefferson's initials etched on the glass.

# TOP FIVE WORLD'S MOST MICHELIN-STARRED CHEFS*

| | CHEF | COUNTRY | NO. OF MICHELIN STARS |
|---|---|---|---|
| 1 | **Joël Robuchon** | **France** | **25** |
| 2 | Alain Ducasse | France | 21 |
| =3 | Gordon Ramsay | UK | 7 |
| =3 | Thomas Keller | USA | 7 |
| 5 | Heston Blumenthal | UK | 6 |

\* As of 2015

# TOP TEN MOST COMMON FOOD ALLERGIES

| 1 | **Cow's milk** |
|---|---|
| 2 | Wheat and other grains with gluten |
| 3 | Soya beans |
| 4 | Yeast |
| 5 | Egg whites |
| 6 | Peanuts |
| 7 | Tree nuts (cashew, almonds, pecans, walnuts, etc.) |
| 8 | Fish |
| 9 | Shellfish |
| 10 | Sesame and sunflower seeds |

# TOP TEN MOST ANTIOXIDANT-RICH FRUITS

| 1 | **Prunes** |
|---|---|
| 2 | Raisins |
| 3 | Blueberries |
| 4 | Blackberries |
| 5 | Strawberries |
| 6 | Raspberries |
| 7 | Plums |
| 8 | Oranges |
| 9 | Red grapes |
| 10 | Cherries |

 # TOP TEN MOST ANTIOXIDANT-RICH VEGETABLES

| 1 | **Kale** |
|---|---|
| 2 | Spinach |
| 3 | Brussels sprouts |
| 4 | Alfalfa sprouts |
| 5 | Broccoli |
| 6 | Beetroot |
| 7 | Red sweet peppers |
| 8 | Onions |
| 9 | Corn |
| 10 | Aubergine |

# TOP TEN MOST TOXIC FRUIT AND VEGETABLES AFTER PESTICIDE USE*

| 1 | Strawberries |
|---|---|
| 2 | Apples |
| 3 | Nectarines |
| 4 | Peaches |
| 5 | Celery |
| 6 | Grapes |
| 7 | Cherries |
| 8 | Spinach |
| 9 | Tomatoes |
| 10 | Sweet peppers |

* From the Environmental Working Group's 2016 Dirty Dozen List
(www.ewg.org)

**Fascinating Facts**

- Iceberg lettuce got its name when California growers started to ship it covered with heaps of crushed ice in the 1920s. It had previously been called 'crisphead' lettuce.

- Archaeologists have found petrified fried cakes with holes in them – very much like the modern doughnut – in prehistoric Native American ruins. Our ancestors had a sweet tooth too!

# TOP TEN WORLD'S BIGGEST FAST-FOOD CHAINS*

| | CHAIN | NO. OF STORES |
|---|---|---|
| **1** | **Subway** | **44,600+** |
| 2 | McDonald's | 36,000+ |
| 3 | Starbucks | 23,000+ |
| 4 | KFC | 19,400+ |
| 5 | Burger King | 14,300+ |
| 6 | Pizza Hut | 14,100+ |
| 7 | Domino's Pizza | 12,900 |
| 8 | Dunkin' Donuts | 9,200 |
| =9 | Baskin-Robbins | 7,300+ |
| =9 | Hunt Brothers Pizza | 7,300+ |

* As of October 2016

# TOP TEN WORLD'S MOST GROWN CROPS

| | CROP | NO. OF MILLION METRIC TONS PRODUCED ANNUALLY |
|---|---|---|
| **1** | **Sugar cane** | **1,324** |
| 2 | Maize | 721 |
| 3 | Wheat | 627 |
| 4 | Rice | 605 |
| 5 | Potatoes | 328 |
| 6 | Sugar beet | 249 |
| 7 | Soya beans | 204 |
| 8 | Oil palm | 162 |
| 9 | Barley | 154 |
| 10 | Tomatoes | 120 |

# TOP TEN BRITAIN'S BIGGEST GROCERY BRANDS*

| 1 | Coca Cola |
|---|---|
| 2 | Warburtons |
| 3 | Walkers |
| 4 | Cadbury Dairy Milk |
| 5 | Birds Eye |
| 6 | McVitie's |
| 7 | Lucozade |
| 8 | Nescafé |
| 9 | Pepsi |
| 10 | Kingsmill |

* As of 2015

## Fascinating Fact

- Teabags were invented in 1904 by Thomas Sullivan in New York; he first used them to send samples to his customers instead of sealing the tea leaves in more expensive tins.

# TOP TEN BESTSELLING CHOCOLATES IN THE UK*

| | |
|---|---|
| 1 | **Cadbury Dairy Milk** |
| 2 | Galaxy |
| 3 | Maltesers |
| 4 | Kinder |
| 5 | KitKat |
| 6 | Snickers |
| 7 | Wispa |
| 8 | Mars |
| 9 | Twirl |
| 10 | Aero |

\* As of September 2015

# TOP TEN WORLD'S BIGGEST CHOCOLATE CONSUMERS

| | COUNTRY | ANNUAL AMOUNT CONSUMED PER PERSON |
|---|---|---|
| 1 | **Switzerland** | **8.9 kg** |
| 2 | Germany | 7.8 kg |
| =3 | Ireland | 7.4 kg |
| =3 | UK | 7.4 kg |
| 5 | Norway | 6.6 kg |
| 6 | Sweden | 5.4 kg |
| 7 | Australia | 4.9 kg |
| 8 | The Netherlands | 4.7 kg |
| 9 | USA | 4.3 kg |
| 10 | France | 4.2 kg |

 **HUNTING SEASONS IN THE UK**

| SEASON | DATES |
|---|---|
| Pheasant | 1 October to 1 February |
| Partridge | 1 September to 1 February |
| Grouse | 12 August to 10 December |
| Duck and goose (inland) | 1 September to 31 January |
| Duck and goose (below high-water mark) | 1 September 20 February |
| Chinese water deer | 1 November to 31 March |
| Red deer stag | 1 August to 30 April |
| Red deer hind | 1 November to 31 March |
| Roe deer buck | 1 April to 31 October |
| Roe deer doe | 1 November to 31 March |

 **TOP TEN WORLD'S BIGGEST EVER FRUITS AND VEGETABLES**

| FRUIT/ VEGETABLE | PLACE GROWN | WEIGHT |
|---|---|---|
| **Pumpkin** | **Pfungen, Switzerland** | **1,056 kg** |
| Watermelon | Tennessee, USA | 159 kg |
| Marrow | Norfolk, UK | 65 kg |
| Cabbage | Rhondda Cynon Taf, Wales | 56.2 kg |
| Jackfruit | Hawaii, USA | 34.6 kg |
| Cauliflower | Alaska, USA | 14.1 kg |
| Sweet potato | Tyre, Lebanon | 11.3 kg |

| Carrot | Alaska, USA | 8.61 kg |
| Lemon | Kfar Zeitim, Israel | 5.3 kg |
| Apple | Hirosaki City, Japan | 1.85 kg |

## Fascinating Facts

- The tallest ever tomato plant reached an astonishing height of almost 20 metres in Lancashire, UK, in 2000.

- Carrots were first cultivated in Afghanistan in the seventh century, and they had yellow flesh and a purple exterior. It was the Dutch who developed the orange carrot in deference to the House of Orange, and the French, in the seventeenth century, who most likely developed the elongated carrot, the precursor to the modern carrot.

 **WORLD'S FASTEST EATERS**

**Joey 'Jaws' Chestnut** – 70 hot dogs (in buns) in 10 minutes

**Patrick 'Deep Dish' Bertoletti** – 468 individual raw oysters in 8 minutes and 16 8-ounce corned-beef sandwiches in 10 minutes

**Takeru 'Tsunami' Kobayashi** – 50 hot dogs in 12 minutes

**Tim 'Eater X' Janus** – 71 tamales in 12 minutes, 26 large cannoli in 6 minutes, 11.8 lb of burritos in 10 minutes, 10.5 lb of ramen noodles in 8 minutes, and 4 lb of tiramisu in 6 minutes

**'Humble' Bob Shoudt** – 9.25 lb of shoefly pie in 8 minutes, 7.6 lb of meatballs in 12 minutes, and 25 hot dogs in 12 minutes

**Sonya 'Black Widow' Thomas** – 11 lb of cheesecake in 9 minutes

**Hall Hunt** – 40 hamburgers and five big Angus burgers in 8 minutes

**'The Lovely' Juliet Lee** – 13 lb of cranberry sauce in 8 minutes

**Tim 'Gravy' Brown** – 10 lb of cucumber and asparagus washed down with a gallon of water in less than 4 minutes

**Richard 'The Locust' LeFevre** – 5 lb of birthday cake in 11 minutes and 26 seconds, and 247 jalapeño peppers in 8 minutes

# MOST DANGEROUS FOODS

**Hot dogs** – to blame for 17 per cent of deaths from choking

**Fugu (pufferfish)** – the internal organs contain a deadly poison

**Ackee** – ingesting the unripe fruit is poisonous, as it causes chronic vomiting that can result in coma or death

**Peanuts** – the most dangerous food for allergy sufferers

**Leafy greens** – unwashed greens sometimes carry norovirus, which causes 300 deaths a year in the USA alone

**Rhubarb** – ingesting a large amount of the leaves can cause poisoning, due to the toxins they contain

**Tuna** – high mercury levels caused by pollution can be dangerous for very young and unborn children

**Tapioca** – prepared incorrectly, the cassava root (where the starch comes from) can produce cyanide

**Coffee** – can cause severe burning if mishandled

**Mushrooms** – varieties such as death cap, destroying angel and deadly webcap are highly poisonous

# TOP TEN FOODS HIGHEST IN SATURATED FAT

| | |
|---|---|
| 1 | **Hydrogenated oils (coconut, palm) – 93 per cent** |
| 2 | Dried coconut – 57 per cent |
| 3 | Rendered animal fats (tallow, suet) – 52 per cent |
| 4 | Butter – 51 per cent |
| 5 | Dark chocolate – 32 per cent |
| 6 | Fish oil (menhaden, sardine) – 20–30 per cent |
| 7 | Cheese – 20 per cent |
| 8 | Nuts and seeds (pili, macadamia) – 9–31 per cent |
| 9 | Processed meats (sausage and pâté) – 15 per cent |
| 10 | Whipped cream – 14 per cent |

## Fascinating Facts

- Vikings used the skulls of their enemies as drinking vessels. *Skol!*

- Absinthe was banned in most countries in the early twentieth century, as it apparently caused madness. The reason was the presence of the toxic oil thujone in wormwood, which was then one of the main ingredients.

# HISTORY

# THE 12 CAESARS

| | NAME | REIGN |
|---|---|---|
| 1 | Julius Caesar (b. 100 BC, d. 44 BC) | 49–44 BC |
| 2 | Augustus (b. 63 BC, d. AD 14) | 27 BC–AD 14 |
| 3 | Tiberius (b. 42 BC, d. AD 37) | AD 14–37 |
| 4 | Gaius Caligula (b. AD 12, d. AD 41) | AD 37–41 |
| 5 | Claudius (b. 10 BC, d. AD 54) | AD 41–54 |
| 6 | Nero (b. AD 37, d. AD 68) | AD 54–68 |
| 7 | Galba (b. 3 BC, d. AD 69) | AD 68–69 |
| 8 | Otho (b. AD 32, d. AD 69) | AD 69 |
| 9 | Vitellius (b. AD 15, d. AD 69) | AD 69 |
| 10 | Vespasian (b. AD 9, d. AD 79) | AD 69–79 |
| 11 | Titus (b. AD 39, d. AD 81) | AD 79–81 |
| 12 | Domitian (b. AD 51, d. AD 96) | AD 81–96 |

# PREHISTORIC PERIODS

| ERA | PREDOMINANT MATERIAL | PERIOD |
|---|---|---|
| Paleolithic (Old Stone Age) | Knapped stone, wood and bone | Approx. 2.5 million to 15,000 years ago |
| Mesolithic (Middle Stone Age) | Flint | Approx. 15,000 to 10,000 years ago |
| Neolithic (New Stone Age) | Polished stone | Approx. 10,000 to 6,000 years ago |
| Bronze Age | Copper and tin alloy | Approx. 6,000 to 4,000 years ago |
| Iron Age | Iron | Approx. 3,000 years ago |

# TOP TEN WORLD'S LONGEST WARS

| | |
|---|---|
| **1** | **Hundred Years' War, France vs England: 1337–1453 (116 years)** |
| 2 | Greco-Persian Wars, Greece vs Persia: 499–449 BC (50 years) |
| =3 | Wars of the Roses, Lancaster vs York: 1455–85 (30 years) |
| =3 | Thirty Years' War, Catholic vs Protestant: 1618–48 (30 years) |
| 5 | Peloponnesian War, Peloponnesian League vs Delian League: 431–404 BC (27 years) |
| =6 | First Punic War, Rome vs Carthage: 264–241 BC (23 years) |
| =6 | Napoleonic Wars, France vs other European countries: 1792–1815 (23 years) |
| 8 | Second Great Northen War, Russia vs Sweden and Baltic states: 1700–21 (21 years) |
| 9 | Vietnam War, South Vietnam (with USA support) vs North Vietnam: 1957–75 (18 years) |
| 10 | Second Punic War, Rome vs Carthage: 218–201 BC (17 years) |

# KNIGHTS OF THE ROUND TABLE*

| | |
|---|---|
| King Arthur | Lamorak |
| Galahad | Bors de Ganis |
| Lancelot du Lac | Safir |
| Gawain | Pelleas |
| Percivale | Kay |
| Lionel | Ector de Maris |
| Tristram de Lyones | Dagonet |
| Gareth | Tegyr |
| Bedivere | Brunor le Noir |
| Bleoberis | Le Bel Desconneu |
| La Cote Male Taile | Alymere |
| Lucan | Mordred |
| Palomides | |

\* Listed from the Winchester Round Table dating from 1270

# TOP FIVE LONGEST SIEGES IN HISTORY

| 1 | Candia, Ottoman Turks besieged the Venetians: 1648–69 (21 years) |
|---|---|
| 2 | Khost, Afghan Mujahideen besieged Soviet Union / Afghanistan: 1980–91 (11 years) |
| 3 | Ishiyama Hongan-ji, forces of Oda Nobunaga besieged Ikkō-ikki: 1570–80 (10 years) |
| 4 | Solovetsky Monastery, Tsar's forces besieged Raskol monks: 1668–76 (8 years) |
| 5 | Harlech Castle, Yorkists besieged Lancastrians: 1461–68 (7 years) |

# TOP TEN WORLD'S LARGEST ARMIES*

| 1 | China – 2,333,000 |
|---|---|
| 2 | USA – 1,433,000 |
| 3 | India – 1,346,000 |
| 4 | North Korea – 1,190,000 |
| 5 | Russia – 771,000 |
| 6 | South Korea – 655,000 |
| 7 | Pakistan – 644,000 |
| 8 | Iran – 523,000 |
| 9 | Turkey – 511,000 |
| 10 | Vietnam – 482,000 |

* As of 2015 – ranked by active-duty personnel

**TOP TEN LARGEST EMPIRES IN HISTORY**

| | EMPIRE | SIZE* |
|---|---|---|
| 1 | **British Empire (1603–1949)** | **13.7 million sq miles (33.5 million sq km)** |
| 2 | Mongol Empire (1206–1368) | 12.7 million sq miles (33 million sq km) |
| 3 | Russian Empire (1721–1917) | 8.8 million sq miles (22.8 million sq km) |
| 4 | Spanish Empire (1492–1975) | 7.7 million sq miles (20 million sq km) |
| 5 | Qing Chinese Empire (1644–1912) | 5.7 million sq miles (14.7 million sq km) |
| 6 | Yuan Dynasty (1271–1368) | 5.4 million sq miles (14 million sq km) |
| 7 | Umayyad Caliphate (AD 661–750) | 5 million sq miles (13 million sq km) |
| 8 | Second French Colonial Empire (1870–1960s) | 4.7 million sq miles (12.3 million sq km) |
| 9 | Abbāsid Caliphate (AD 750–1258) | 4.3 million sq miles (11.1 million sq km) |
| 10 | Portuguese Empire (1415–2002) | 4.2 million sq miles (10.4 million sq km) |

* At the peak of the empire

# FIRST COUNTRIES TO GIVE THE VOTE TO WOMEN

| YEAR | COUNTRY |
|------|---------|
| 1893 | New Zealand |
| 1902 | Australia |
| 1906 | Finland |
| 1913 | Norway |
| 1915 | Denmark and Iceland |
| 1917 | The Netherlands and USSR |
| 1918 | Austria, Germany, Poland, Canada, Great Britain and Ireland |
| 1920 | USA |
| 1921 | Sweden |
| 1929 | Ecuador |

# TOP FIVE LONGEST-REIGNING UK MONARCHS

| | MONARCH | REIGN |
|---|---------|-------|
| 1 | **Queen Elizabeth II** | **February 1952 to present (64 years and counting)** |
| 2 | Queen Victoria | June 1837 to January 1901 (63 years) |
| 3 | George III | October 1760 to January 1820 (59 years) |
| 4 | James VI and I | July 1567 to March 1625 (58 years*) |
| 5 | Henry III | October 1216 to November 1272 (56 years) |

* As James VI of Scotland, he reigned for 58 years, but as James I he ruled England as well for the last 22 years of his reign

MAN FACTS

# LINE OF SUCCESSION TO THE BRITISH THRONE

| | |
|---|---|
| **1** | **HRH Prince Charles, Prince of Wales (b. 1948)** |
| 2 | HRH Prince William, Duke of Cambridge, eldest son of Prince Charles (b. 1982) |
| 3 | HRH Prince George, son of Prince William (b. 2013) |
| 4 | HRH Princess Charlotte, daughter of Prince William (b. 2015) |
| 5 | HRH Prince Henry of Wales (Prince Harry), youngest son of Prince Charles (b. 1984) |
| 6 | HRH Prince Andrew, The Duke of York, second son of HM Queen Elizabeth II (b. 1960) |
| 7 | HRH Princess Beatrice of York, eldest daughter of Prince Andrew (b. 1988) |
| 8 | HRH Princess Eugenie of York, youngest daughter of Prince Andrew (b. 1990) |
| 9 | HRH Prince Edward, Earl of Wessex, youngest son of HM Queen Elizabeth II (b. 1964) |
| 10 | HRH Prince James of Wessex, Viscount Severn, son of Prince Edward (b. 2007) |
| 11 | Lady Louise Alice Elizabeth Mary Mountbatten-Windsor, daughter of Prince Edward (b. 2003) |

# KINGS AND QUEENS OF ENGLAND

| MONARCH | YEAR ASCENDED TO THE THRONE |
|---|---|
| **NORMAN** | |
| William I | 1066 |
| William II | 1087 |
| Henry I | 1100 |
| Stephen | 1135 |
| | |
| **PLANTAGENET** | |
| Henry II | 1154 |
| Richard I | 1189 |
| John | 1199 |
| Henry III | 1216 |
| Edward I | 1272 |
| Edward II | 1307 |
| Edward III | 1327 |
| Richard II | 1377 |
| | |
| **LANCASTER** | |
| Henry IV | 1399 |
| Henry V | 1413 |
| Henry VI | 1422 |
| | |
| **YORK** | |
| Edward IV | 1461 |
| Edward V | 1483 |
| Richard III | 1483 |

## TUDOR

| | |
|---|---|
| Henry VII | 1485 |
| Henry VIII | 1509 |
| Edward VI | 1547 |
| Mary I | 1553 |
| Elizabeth I | 1558 |

## STUART

| | |
|---|---|
| James I | 1603 |
| Charles I | 1625 |
| The Interregnum | 1649 |
| Charles II | 1660 |
| James II | 1685 |
| William III and Mary II | 1688 |
| Anne | 1702 |

## HANOVER

| | |
|---|---|
| George I | 1714 |
| George II | 1727 |
| George III | 1760 |
| George IV | 1820 |
| William IV | 1830 |
| Victoria | 1837 |

## SAXE-COBURG AND GOTHA

| | |
|---|---|
| Edward VII | 1901 |

## WINDSOR

| | |
|---|---|
| George V | 1910 |
| Edward VIII | 1936 |
| George VI | 1936 |
| Elizabeth II | 1952 |

# A VERSE TO HELP REMEMBER ALL THIS

Willie, Willie, Harry, Stee,

Harry, Dick, John, Harry three;

Edwards one, two, three, Dick two,

Henrys four, five, six... then who?

Edwards four, five, Dick the bad,

Harrys (twain), Ned six (the lad);

Mary, Lizzie, James the Vain,

Then Charlie, Charlie, James again...

William and Mary, Anna Gloria,

Georges four, Will four, Victoria;

Eddie seven, Georgie five, Ned the eighth;

George the sixth, Elizabeth.

# KEY DATES IN BRITISH HISTORY

| DATES (AD) | EVENT |
| --- | --- |
| 43 | Roman Emperor Claudius invades Britain |
| 61 | Revolt by Queen Boudicca of the Iceni tribe against the Romans |
| 122–26 | Construction of Hadrian's Wall |
| 435 | Britain invaded by Angles, Saxons and Jutes |
| 597 | St Augustine lands in Kent (AD 602 founds Canterbury Cathedral and becomes first Archbishop of Canterbury) |
| 782–3 | Construction of Offa's Dyke |
| 793 | First Viking raid on Britain |

| DATES (AD) | EVENT |
| --- | --- |
| 823 | Egbert, King of Wessex, acknowledged as overlord of all England |
| 1040 | Macbeth slays Duncan |
| 1066 | William the Conqueror defeats Harold Godwinson at the Battle of Hastings and is crowned king |
| 1086 | Domesday Book completed |
| 1170 | Murder of Thomas à Beckett in the Canterbury Cathedral |
| 1215 | King John signs the Magna Carta at Runnymede, 15 June |
| 1216 | Llywelyn the Great is de facto ruler of Wales |
| 1314 | Robert Bruce defeats the English |
| 1415 | Battle of Agincourt, victory for Henry V |
| 1453 | End of Hundred Years' War (1337–1453) |
| 1485 | End of Battle of Bosworth Field (Wars of the Roses 1455–85) |
| 1513 | Battle of Flodden (James IV of Scotland killed) |
| 1536 | Anne Boleyn executed and Thomas Cromwell dissolves monasteries |
| 1587 | Execution of Mary, Queen of Scots |
| 1588 | Spanish Armada defeated |
| 1611 | King James Bible (authorised version of the Bible) completed |
| 1642 | English Civil War begins, Battle of Edgehill |
| 1645 | Battle of Naseby |
| 1649 | Charles I executed |
| 1660 | Restoration of monarchy under Charles II |
| 1665 | Great Plague of London |
| 1666 | Great Fire of London |
| 1690 | Battle of the Boyne (James II defeated in Ireland) |
| 1692 | Massacre of Glencoe |
| 1707 | Act of Union |
| 1746 | Battle of Culloden Moor |
| 1775 | American War of Independence |

| DATES (AD) | EVENT |
| --- | --- |
| 1801 | Union of Great Britain and Ireland |
| 1807 | Slave trade abolished in British Empire |
| 1825 | First railway opened, Stockton to Darlington |
| 1834 | Tolpuddle Martyrs deported to Australia for seven years |
| 1840 | Penny Postage instituted; Opium War against China declared |
| 1851 | Great Exhibition in the Crystal Palace, Hyde Park |
| 1854 | Charge of the Light Brigade during Crimean War |
| 1857 | Indian Mutiny, Relief of Lucknow |
| 1879 | Zulu War; Tay Bridge disaster |
| 1899 | Boer War |
| 1914 | Franz Ferdinand assassinated at Sarajevo and World War One begins |
| 1916 | Battles of Verdun, Jutland and the Somme |
| 1918 | Armistice Day; women over 30 get the vote |
| 1921 | Irish Free State declared |
| 1939 | Germany invades Poland and World War Two begins |
| 1940 | Dunkirk evacuated; Battle of Britain |
| 1944 | D-Day landings by Allies, 6 June |
| 1945 | World War Two ends |
| 1952 | George VI dies; Princess Elizabeth accedes to the throne |
| 1953 | Edmund Hillary and Sherpa Tenzing reach Everest summit |
| 1954 | Food rationing ends in UK |
| 1964 | Last man hanged in UK |
| 1971 | Decimalisation of currency |
| 1973 | Britain joins the Common Market |
| 1982 | Falklands War begins |
| 1990 | Margaret Thatcher resigns as Prime Minister after 11 years and 209 days in office |
| 1991 | First Gulf War begins in Iraq |
| 1994 | Official opening of the Channel Tunnel |
| 1997 | Diana, Princess of Wales, killed in car crash |

| DATES (AD) | EVENT |
| --- | --- |
| 1998 | The Good Friday Agreement |
| 2002 | The Queen Mother dies, aged 101 |
| 2003 | Second Gulf War in Iraq |
| 2005 | Terrorists explode bombs on London Transport System |
| 2007 | Elizabeth II becomes the oldest reigning British monarch |
| 2008 | Boris Johnson becomes new Mayor of London |
| 2010 | First coalition government since 1945 |
| 2012 | London Olympics |
| 2016 | United Kingdom votes to leave the EU |

# THE SEVEN WONDERS OF THE ANCIENT WORLD*

| 1 | **Pyramids, Giza** |
| --- | --- |
| 2 | Hanging Gardens of Babylon |
| 3 | Temple of Artemis, Ephesus |
| 4 | Statue of Zeus, Olympia |
| 5 | Mausoleum at Halicarnassus |
| 6 | Colossus of Rhodes |
| 7 | Pharos Lighthouse, Alexandria |

* Only the Pyramids can still be seen today

# EVOLUTION OF THE 'HOMO' SPECIES

*Homo habilis* ('handy man'): 2.5–1.5 million years ago

*Homo rudolfensis* ('rudolph man'): 1.9 million years ago

*Homo georgicus* ('Georgia man'): 1.8–1.6 million years ago

*Homo ergaster* (working man'): 1.9–1.25 million years

*Homo erectus* ('upright man'): *c.* 1.25–0.3 million years ago

*Homo cepranensis* ('ceprano man'): *c.* 0.8 million years ago

*Homo antecessor* ('predecessor man'): 0.8–0.35 million years ago

*Homo heidelbergensis* ('Heidelberg man'): 0.67–0.25 million years ago

*Homo neanderthalensis* ('Neanderthal man'): 0.23–0.03 million years ago

*Homo rhodesiensis* ('Rhodesia man'): 0.3–0.12 million years ago

*Homo sapiens idaltu* ('elderly wise man'): 0.16 million years ago

*Homo floresiensis* ('Flores man'): 0.10–0.012 million years ago

*Homo sapiens*: 0.25 million years ago to present

## Fascinating Facts

- The Battle of Hastings did not take place in Hastings, but was actually fought at Senlac Hill, about 6 miles north-west of Hastings.

- In Ancient Egypt, the heart was considered to be the seat of intelligence – not the brain.

- During the past 3,500 years, it is estimated that the world has had a grand total of 230 years in which no wars took place.

- In Ancient Egypt, cats were considered sacred. When a family pet cat died, the entire family would shave off their eyebrows and remain in mourning until they had grown back.

# LANGUAGE

# TOP TEN MOST WIDELY SPOKEN LANGUAGES

| | LANGUAGE | NATIVE SPEAKERS |
|---|---|---|
| 1 | **Mandarin** | **960 million** |
| 2 | Spanish | 548 million |
| 3 | Hindi | 545 million |
| 4 | Arabic | 420 million |
| 5 | English | 359 million* |
| 6 | Russian | 260 million |
| 7 | Portuguese | 220 million |
| 8 | Bengali | 210 million |
| 9 | Japanese | 125 million |
| 10 | German | 100 million |

* English is the official language of 54 countries but as many as a billion people have learnt it as an additional language

# TOP TEN WORLD'S MOST DIFFICULT LANGUAGES

| 1 | Tuyuca, eastern Amazon – 50–140 noun classes or genders |
|---|---|
| 2 | Kwaio, central Malaita, Solomon Islands |
| 3 | !Xóõ or Taa, Botswana and Namibia – a Khoisan language with 17 vowel sounds and five basic clicks |
| 4 | Ubykh, Manyas, Turkey – 78 consonant sounds; now a dead language |
| 5 | Bora, Peru and Colombia – 350 noun classes or genders |
| 6 | Chindali, Tanzania and Malawi – a Bantu language |
| 7 | Berik, New Guinea – belongs to the Tor-Kwerba language. |
| 8 | Kuuk-Thaayorre, North Australia – a Paman language; only 250 speakers in 2006 |
| 9 | Dyirbal, Queensland, Australia – branch of the Pama-Nyungan family; possibly fewer than five speakers |
| 10 | Estonian – 14 cases of grammar |

# TOP TEN PANGRAMS*

| =1 | Waltz, bad nymph, for quick jigs vex. (28 letters) |
|---|---|
| =1 | Brick quiz whangs jumpy veldt fox. (28 letters) |
| =3 | Quick zephyrs blow, vexing daft Jim. (29 letters) |
| =3 | Sphinx of black quartz, judge my vow. (29 letters) |
| 5 | Two driven jocks help fax my big quiz. (30 letters) |
| =6 | Five quacking zephyrs jolt my wax bed. (31 letters) |
| =6 | The five boxing wizards jump quickly. (31 letters) |
| 8 | Pack my box with five dozen liquor jugs. (32 letters) |
| 9 | The quick brown fox jumps over the lazy dog. (35 letters) |
| 10 | Jinxed wizards pluck ivy from the big quilt. (36 letters) |

* A sentence that includes every letter of the alphabet at least once

# RECENT ADDITIONS TO THE DICTIONARY*

**glamping** – camping in style

**starchitect** – a famous architect whose designs are considered extravagant or outlandish

**bovver** – variant of bother

**vlog** – a blog composed of posts in video form

**listicles** – online newspaper or magazine articles presented in the form of lists

**dudette** – a female dude

**phubbing** – ignoring companions in order to pay attention to a phone or mobile device

**athleisure** – casual clothing designed to be worn for exercising as well as general use

**budgie smugglers** – tight-fitting male swimming trunks

**nomophobia** – fear of being out of mobile-phone contact

\* Words added to British and American dictionaries in 2016

 # TOP TEN MOST COMMONLY USED WORDS IN THE ENGLISH LANGUAGE

| 1 | the |
|---|-----|
| 2 | of |
| 3 | to |
| 4 | and |
| 5 | a |
| 6 | in |
| 7 | is |
| 8 | it |
| 9 | you |
| 10 | that |

# COLLECTORS AND COLLECTIONS

| COLLECTOR | COLLECTION |
| --- | --- |
| Arctophile | Teddy bears |
| Bibliophile | Books |
| Campanarian | Bells |
| Cartophilist | Cigarette cards |
| Cochlearist | Spoons |
| Conchologist | Shells |
| Deltiologist | Postcards |
| Digitabulist | Thimbles |
| Fromologist | Cheese labels |
| Grabatologist | Ties |
| Lepidopterist | Butterflies/moths |
| Numismatist | Coins |
| Philatelist | Stamps |
| Phillumenist | Matchbox labels |
| Tegestologist | Beer mats |
| Vintitulist | Wine labels |

 # THE GREEK ALPHABET

| | | |
|---|---|---|
| A α: Alpha | Λ λ: Lambda | Φ φ: Phi |
| B β: Beta | M μ: Mu | X χ: Chi |
| Γ γ: Gamma | N ν: Nu | Ψ ψ: Psi |
| Δ δ: Delta | Ξ ξ: Xi | Ω ω: Omega |
| E ε: Epsilon | O ο: Omicron | |
| Z ζ: Zeta | Π π: Pi | |
| H η: Eta | P ρ: Rho | |
| Θ θ: Theta | Σ σ: Sigma | |
| I ι: Iota | T τ: Tau | |
| K κ: Kappa | Y υ: Upsilon | |

 # THE PHONETIC ALPHABET

| | | | | |
|---|---|---|---|---|
| Alpha | Golf | Mike | Sierra | Yankee |
| Bravo | Hotel | November | Tango | Zulu |
| Charlie | India | Oscar | Uniform | |
| Delta | Juliet | Papa | Victor | |
| Echo | Kilo | Quebec | Whiskey | |
| Foxtrot | Lima | Romeo | X-ray | |

# LANGUAGE FAMILIES AND NUMBER OF SPEAKERS

| LANGUAGE FAMILIES | NO. OF SPEAKERS |
| --- | --- |
| Indo-European | 2,910,000,000 |
| Sino-Tibetan | 1,268,000,000 |
| Niger-Congo | 437,000,000 |
| Austronesian | 386,000,000 |
| Afro-Asiatic | 380,000,000 |
| Dravidian | 229,000,000 |
| Altaic | 150,000,000 |
| Japonic | 129,000,000 |
| Austro-Asiatic | 80,000,000 |
| Tai | 80,000,000 |
| Korean | 77,000,000 |
| Amerindian (North, Central, South America) | 45,000,000 |
| Nilo-Saharan | 30,000,000 |
| Uralic | 22,000,000 |
| Miao-Yao | 7,000,000 |
| Caucasian | 6,000,000 |
| Indo-Pacific | 3,000,000 |
| Khoisan | 50,000 |
| Australian aborigine | 50,000 |
| Paleosiberian | 23,000 |

# LATIN PHRASES COMMONLY USED IN ENGLISH

| LATIN PHRASE | ENGLISH TRANSLATION |
| --- | --- |
| Ad hoc | 'towards this', for this special purpose |
| Ad infinitum | 'to infinity', endless repetition |
| Ad nauseam | 'to the point of sickness', endlessly repetitive |
| A priori | 'from the previous', deductive reasoning |
| Bona fides | 'good faith', genuineness |
| Carpe diem | 'seize the day', enjoy the moment |
| Compos mentis | 'having control of one's mind', sane |
| Curriculum vitae | 'course of life', outline of qualifications and experience |
| Et al | 'and other things' |
| Ex gratia | 'from favour', given as a favour |
| Habeas corpus | 'you should have the body', maintains the right of the subject to protection from unlawful imprisonment |
| In camera | 'in the room', secret |
| In extremis | 'in the last', in desperate circumstances |
| In flagrante delecto | 'with the crime blazing', actually committing the crime |
| Infra dig | 'below dignity', below one's dignity |
| In loco parentis | 'in place of a parent' |
| In vitro | 'in glass', in a test tube |
| Ipso facto | 'by the fact itself', thereby |
| Mea culpa | 'through my fault', expression of repentance |
| Non sequitur | 'it does not follow', an illogical step in an argument |
| Nota bene | 'note well', often abbreviated as NB |
| Per capita | 'by heads', per head of the population |
| Prima facie | 'at first sight', on the evidence available |
| Quid pro quo | 'something for something', retaliation |
| Quod erat demonstrandum | 'which was to be shown', often used as QED |
| Sine qua non | 'without which not', an indispensable condition |

 **PHOBIAS**

| | |
|---|---|
| Acrophobia | Fear of heights |
| Agoraphobia | Fear of open spaces |
| Ailourophobia | Fear of cats |
| Algophobia | Fear of pain |
| Androphobia | Fear of men |
| Apiphobia | Fear of bees |
| Arachnophobia | Fear of spiders |
| Astraphobia | Fear of lightning |
| Bibliophobia | Fear of books |
| Brontophobia | Fear of thunder |
| Claustrophobia | Fear of enclosed spaces |
| Cynophobia | Fear of dogs |
| Dendrophobia | Fear of trees |
| Ergasiophobia | Fear of work |
| Gametophobia | Fear of marriage |
| Gymnophobia | Fear of nudity |
| Gynophobia | Fear of women |
| Haematophobia | Fear of blood |
| Hippophobia | Fear of horses |
| Hydrophobia | Fear of water |
| Lalophobia | Fear of speech |
| Linonophobia | Fear of string |
| Musophobia | Fear of mice |
| Nosophobia | Fear of disease |
| Nyctophobia | Fear of darkness |
| Ombrophobia | Fear of rain |
| Oneirophobia | Fear of dreams |
| Ophidiophobia | Fear of snakes |
| Ornithophobia | Fear of birds |
| Phasmophobia | Fear of ghosts |
| Phonophobia | Fear of noise / speaking aloud |
| Pteraphobia | Fear of flying |

| Pyrophobia | Fear of fire |
|---|---|
| Sciophobia | Fear of shadows |
| Teratophobia | Fear of monsters |
| Triskaidekaphobia | Fear of the number 13 |
| Xenophobia | Fear of foreigners |
| Zoophobia | Fear of animals |

## Fascinating Facts

- There are more than 2,700 spoken languages in the world. In addition, there are more than 7,000 dialects.

- All pilots on international flights identify themselves in English.

- Somalia is the only African country in which the entire population speaks the same language: Somali.

- More than 1,000 different languages are spoken on the continent of Africa. Many languages in Africa include a 'click' sound that is pronounced at the same time as other sounds.

# LITERATURE

# TOP TEN BESTSELLING BOOKS OF ALL TIME*

| | TITLE | AUTHOR | NO. OF COPIES SOLD |
|---|---|---|---|
| 1 | *The Holy Qur'an* | | **Over 3 billion** |
| 2 | *The King James Bible* | | Over 2.5 billion |
| 3 | *Quotations from Chairman Mao Tse-tung* | Mao Tse-tung | 800 million |
| 4 | *Don Quixote* | Miguel de Cervantes | 500 million |
| 5 | *A Tale of Two Cities* | Charles Dickens | 200 million |
| =6 | *The Lord of the Rings* | J. R. R. Tolkien | 150 million |
| =6 | *The Book of Mormon* | Joseph Smith Jr | 150 million |
| 8 | *Le Petit Prince* | Antoine de Saint-Exupéry | 140 million |
| 9 | *Harry Potter and the Philosopher's Stone* | J. K. Rowling | 107 million |
| 10 | *And Then There Were None* | Agatha Christie | 100 million |

* As of 2016

# TOP TEN MOST TRANSLATED AUTHORS*

| 1 | **Agatha Christie** |
|---|---|
| 2 | Jules Verne |
| 3 | William Shakespeare |
| 4 | Enid Blyton |
| 5 | Barbara Cartland |
| 6 | Danielle Steel |
| 7 | Vladimir Lenin |
| 8 | Hans Christian Andersen |
| 9 | Stephen King |
| 10 | Jacob Grimm |

* As of 2015

# TOP TEN BESTSELLING BOOKS IN THE UK IN 2015

| | TITLE | AUTHOR | NO. OF COPIES SOLD |
|---|---|---|---|
| 1 | *Grey: Fifty Shades of Grey as Told by Christian* | **E. L. James** | **1,075,206** |
| 2 | *Grandpa's Great Escape* | David Walliams | 532,513 |
| 3 | *The Girl on the Train* | Paula Hawkins | 477,887 |
| 4 | *Millie Marotta's Animal Kingdom* | Millie Marotta | 409,858 |
| 5 | *Mog's Christmas Calamity* | Judith Kerr | 382,014 |
| 6 | *Elizabeth is Missing* | Emma Healey | 368,786 |
| 7 | *Go Set a Watchman* | Harper Lee | 342,146 |
| 8 | *The Miniaturist* | Jessie Burton | 320,648 |
| 9 | *Diary of a Wimpy Kid: Old School* | Jeff Kinney | 313,640 |
| 10 | *Guinness World Records 2015* | Guinness World Records | 309,900 |

# TOP TEN MOST BORROWED AUTHORS IN THE UK*

| 1 | James Patterson |
|---|---|
| 2 | Julia Donaldson |
| 3 | Daisy Meadows |
| 4 | Francesca Simon |
| 5 | M. C. Beaton |
| 6 | Adam Blade |
| 7 | Nora Roberts |
| 8 | Jacqueline Wilson |
| 9 | Lee Child |
| 10 | Anna Jacobs |

\* Based on data from July 2014 to June 2015

# TOP TEN BESTSELLING AUTHORS OF ALL TIME*

| =1 | William Shakespeare | 4 billion |
|---|---|---|
| =1 | Agatha Christie | 4 billion |
| 3 | Barbara Cartland | 1 billion |
| 4 | Danielle Steel | 800 million |
| 5 | Harold Robbins | 750 million |
| 6 | Georges Simenon | 700 million |
| =7 | Sidney Sheldon | 600 million |
| =7 | Enid Blyton | 600 million |
| =9 | Dr Seuss | 500 million |
| =9 | Gilbert Patten | 500 million |

\* Based on maximum estimated copies sold. For some authors, no reliable estimate is available

# TOP TEN MOST BANNED LITERARY CLASSICS

| | TITLE | AUTHOR | REASONS FOR BANNING |
|---|---|---|---|
| **1** | **Ulysses** | **James Joyce** | **Obscenity** |
| 2 | *The Adventures of Huckleberry Finn* | Mark Twain | Racial depictions |
| 3 | *Candide* | Voltaire | Obscenity |
| 4 | *Brave New World* | Aldous Huxley | Presentation of drugs and promiscuity, and its general dystopian outlook |
| 5 | *1984* | George Orwell | Political views and dystopian theme |
| 6 | *The Catcher in the Rye* | J. D. Salinger | Profanity and portrayal of teenage sexuality and angst |
| 7 | *Of Mice and Men* | John Steinbeck | For many reasons, but often cited are its apparent sexism and racism, and its pro-euthanasia and liberal stance |
| 8 | *Slaughterhouse-Five* | Kurt Vonnegut | Controversial subject matter and profanity |
| 9 | *Uncle Tom's Cabin* | Harriet B. Stowe | Anti-slavery stance |
| 10 | *Lord of the Flies* | William Golding | Portrayal of the disintegration of human morals, and religion |

# TOP TEN NOVELISTIC ONE-HIT WONDERS

|    | AUTHOR | TITLE |
|----|--------|-------|
| **1** | **Margaret Mitchell** | ***Gone with the Wind*** |
| 2  | Emily Brontë | *Wuthering Heights* |
| 3  | J. D. Salinger | *Catcher in the Rye* |
| 4  | Oscar Wilde | *The Picture of Dorian Gray* |
| 5  | John Kennedy Toole | *A Confederacy of Dunces* |
| 6  | Sylvia Plath | *The Bell Jar* |
| 7  | Anna Sewell | *Black Beauty* |
| 8  | Boris Pasternak | *Dr Zhivago* |
| 9  | Arundhati Roy | *The God of Small Things* |
| 10 | Ralph Waldo Ellison | *Invisible Man* |

# LITERARY FIRSTS

**The first novel**, called *The Tale of Genji*, was written in 1007 by Japanese noblewoman Murasaki Shikibu.

**The first edition of Samuel Johnson's pioneering English dictionary** was published in 1755.

**The first novel submitted to a publisher as a typewritten manuscript** was *Life on the Mississippi* by Mark Twain, published in 1883.

**The first printed book**, a copy of the Buddhist *Diamond Sutra*, was produced in China in 868 using carved wooden blocks to print the text on paper.

# BOOKER PRIZE WINNERS (UK)*

| YEAR | AUTHOR | BOOK TITLE |
| --- | --- | --- |
| 1980 | William Golding | *Rites of Passage* |
| 1981 | Salman Rushdie | *Midnight's Children* |
| 1982 | Thomas Keneally | *Schindler's Ark* |
| 1983 | J. M. Coetzee | *Life and Times of Michael K* |
| 1984 | Anita Brookner | *Hotel du Lac* |
| 1985 | Keri Hulme | *The Bone People* |
| 1986 | Kingsley Amis | *The Old Devils* |
| 1987 | Penelope Lively | *Moon Tiger* |
| 1988 | Peter Carey | *Oscar and Lucinda* |
| 1989 | Kazuo Ishiguro | *The Remains of the Day* |
| 1990 | A. S. Byatt | *Possession* |
| 1991 | Ben Okri | *The Famished Road* |

| YEAR | AUTHOR | BOOK TITLE |
| --- | --- | --- |
| 1992 | Barry Unsworth | *Sacred Hunger* |
| | Michael Ondaatje | *The English Patient* |
| 1993 | Roddy Doyle | *Paddy Clarke Ha Ha Ha* |
| 1994 | James Kelman | *How Late It Was, How Late* |
| 1995 | Pat Barker | *The Ghost Road* |
| 1996 | Graham Swift | *Last Orders* |
| 1997 | Arundhati Roy | *The God of Small Things* |
| 1998 | Ian McEwan | *Amsterdam* |
| 1999 | J. M. Coetzee | *Disgrace* |
| 2000 | Margaret Atwood | *The Blind Assassin* |
| 2001 | Peter Carey | *True History of the Kelly Gang* |
| 2002* | Yann Martel | *Life of Pi* |
| 2003 | DBC Pierre | *Vernon God Little* |
| 2004 | Alan Hollinghurst | *The Line of Beauty* |
| 2005 | John Banville | *The Sea* |
| 2006 | Kiran Desai | *The Inheritance of Loss* |
| 2007 | Anne Enright | *The Gathering* |
| 2008 | Aravind Adiga | *The White Tiger* |
| 2009 | Hilary Mantel | *Wolf Hall* |
| 2010 | Howard Jacobson | *The Finkler Question* |
| 2011 | Julian Barnes | *The Sense of an Ending* |
| 2012 | Hilary Mantel | *Bring Up the Bodies* |
| 2013 | Eleanor Catton | *The Luminaries* |
| 2014 | Richard Flanagan | *Road to the Deep North* |
| 2015 | Marlon James | *A Brief History of Seven Killings* |
| 2016 | Paul Beatty | *The Sellout* |

* From 2002 The Booker Prize became The Man Booker Prize

# PULITZER PRIZE FOR FICTION WINNERS (US)

| YEAR | AUTHOR | BOOK TITLE |
|------|--------|------------|
| 1980 | Norman Mailer | *The Executioner's Song* |
| 1981 | John Kennedy Toole | *A Confederacy of Dunces* |
| 1982 | John Updike | *Rabbit Is Rich* |
| 1983 | Alice Walker | *The Color Purple* |
| 1984 | William Kennedy | *Ironweed* |
| 1985 | Alison Lurie | *Foreign Affairs* |
| 1986 | Larry McMurtry | *Lonesome Dove* |
| 1987 | Peter Taylor | *A Summons to Memphis* |
| 1988 | Toni Morrison | *Beloved* |
| 1989 | Anne Tyler | *Breathing Lessons* |
| 1990 | Oscar Hijuelos | *The Mambo Kings Play Songs of Love* |
| 1991 | John Updike | *Rabbit at Rest* |
| 1992 | Jane Smiley | *A Thousand Acres* |
| 1993 | Robert Olen Butler | *A Good Scent from a Strange Mountain* |
| 1994 | E. Annie Proulx | *The Shipping News* |
| 1995 | Carol Shields | *The Stone Diaries* |
| 1996 | Richard Ford | *Independence Day* |
| 1997 | Steven Millhauser | *Martin Dressler: The Tale of an American Dreamer* |
| 1998 | Philip Roth | *American Pastoral* |
| 1999 | Michael Cunningham | *The Hours* |
| 2000 | Jhumpa Lahiri | *Interpreter of Maladies* |
| 2001 | Michael Chabon | *The Amazing Adventures of Kavalier & Clay* |
| 2002 | Richard Russo | *Empire Falls* |
| 2003 | Jeffrey Eugenides | *Middlesex* |

| YEAR | AUTHOR | BOOK TITLE |
| --- | --- | --- |
| 2004 | Edward P. Jones | *The Known World* |
| 2005 | Marilynne Robinson | *Gilead* |
| 2006 | Geraldine Brooks | *March* |
| 2007 | Cormac McCarthy | *The Road* |
| 2008 | Junot Diaz | *The Brief Wondrous Life of Oscar Wao* |
| 2009 | Elizabeth Strout | *Olive Kitteridge* |
| 2010 | Paul Harding | *Tinkers* |
| 2011 | Jennifer Egan | *A Visit from the Goon Squad* |
| 2012 | No award given | |
| 2013 | Adam Johnson | *The Orphan Master's Son* |
| 2014 | Donna Tartt | *The Goldfinch* |
| 2015 | Anthony Doerr | *All the Light We Cannot See* |
| 2016 | Viet Thanh Nguyen | *The Sympathizer* |

# POETS LAUREATE (UK)*

| YEAR APPOINTED | POET |
| --- | --- |
| 1617 | Ben Jonson |
| 1638 | William D'Avenant |
| 1668 | John Dryden |
| 1689 | Thomas Shadwell |
| 1692 | Nahum Tate |
| 1715 | Nicholas Rowe |
| 1718 | Laurence Eusden |
| 1730 | Colley Cibber |

| YEAR APPOINTED | POET |
| --- | --- |
| 1757 | William Whitehead |
| 1785 | Thomas Warton |
| 1790 | Henry Pye |
| 1813 | Robert Southey |
| 1843 | William Wordsworth |
| 1850 | Alfred Lord Tennyson |
| 1896 | Alfred Austin |
| 1913 | Robert Bridges |
| 1930 | John Masefield |
| 1968 | Cecil Day-Lewis |
| 1972 | John Betjeman |
| 1984 | Ted Hughes |
| 1999 | Andrew Motion |
| 2009 | Carol Ann Duffy |

\* Post not officially established until 1668

# REFUSALS OF THE POETS LAUREATE

| YEAR | POET |
| --- | --- |
| 1757 | Thomas Gray |
| 1785 | William Mason |
| 1813 | Walter Scott |
| 1896 | William Morris |
| 1984 | Philip Larkin |

# LITERARY PSEUDONYMS

| PSEUDONYM | REAL NAME |
| --- | --- |
| Agatha Christie | Mary Westmacott |
| Anne Rice | Howard Allen O'Brien |
| Artemus Ward | Charles Farrar Browne |
| Barbara Cartland | Barbara McCorquodale |
| Barbara Vine or Ruth Rendell | Ruth Barbara Grasemann |
| Boz | Charles Dickens |
| Daniel Defoe | Daniel Foe |
| Dr Seuss | Theodor Seuss Geisel |
| Ed McBain | Evan Hunter |
| E. L. James | Erika Mitchell |
| Elizabeth Peters | Barbara Mertz |
| George Eliot | Mary Ann Evans |
| George Orwell | Eric Arthur Blair |
| George Sand | Amandine-Aurore Lucile Dupin |
| Harold Robbins | Harold Rubin |
| Jack Higgins | Harry Patterson |
| Jack London | John Griffith |
| James Herriot | James Alfred Wight |
| John Beynon | John Wyndham Parkes Lucas Beynon Harris |
| John le Carré | David John Moore Cornwell |
| John Wyndham | John Wyndham Parkes Lucas Beynon Harris |
| Joseph Conrad | Józef Teodor Konrad Korzeniowski |
| Lewis Carroll | Charles Lutwidge Dodgson |
| Mark Twain | Samuel Langhorne Clemens |
| Mickey Spillane | Frank Morrison |
| Molière | Jean-Baptiste Poquelin |

| PSEUDONYM | REAL NAME |
|---|---|
| Robert Galbraith | J. K. Rowling |
| Stephen King | Richard Bachman |
| Tennessee Williams | Thomas Lanier |
| Tom Stoppard | Tomas Straussler |
| Virgil | Publius Vergilius Maro |
| Voltaire | François-Marie Arouet |
| W. C. Fields | Mahatma Kane Jeeves |
| Woody Allen | Allen Stewart Konigsberg |

 # TOP TEN FAMOUS FIRST LINES

**1** **'All happy families are alike; each unhappy family is unhappy in its own way.'**
**Leo Tolstoy, *Anna Karenina***

2 'It is a truth universally acknowledged that a single man in possession of a good fortune must be in want of a wife.'
Jane Austen, *Pride and Prejudice*

3 'It was the best of times, it was the worst of times...'
Charles Dickens, *A Tale of Two Cities*

4 'Last night I dreamt I went to Manderley again.'
Daphne du Maurier, *Rebecca*

5 'As Gregor Samsa awoke one morning from uneasy dreams, he found himself transformed in his bed into a gigantic insect.'
Franz Kafka, *The Metamorphosis*

6 'It was a bright cold day in April, and the clocks were striking thirteen.'
George Orwell, *1984*

7 'I have just returned from a visit to my landlord – the solitary neighbour that I shall be troubled with.'
Emily Brontë, *Wuthering Heights*

8 ‘Midway in our life's journey, I went astray from the straight road and woke to find myself alone in a dark wood.'
Dante's *Inferno*

9 ‘When shall we three meet again?
In thunder, lightning, or in rain?'
William Shakespeare, *Macbeth*

10 ‘My mother died today, or perhaps it was yesterday.'
Albert Camus, *L'Étranger*

 # TOP TEN BRITAIN'S BEST-LOVED POETS

| 1 | **T. S. Eliot** |
|---|---|
| 2 | John Donne |
| 3 | Benjamin Zephaniah |
| 4 | Wilfred Owen |
| 5 | Philip Larkin |
| 6 | William Blake |
| 7 | W. B. Yeats |
| 8 | John Betjeman |
| 9 | John Keats |
| 10 | Dylan Thomas |

# TOP TEN LONGEST NOVELS
# IN THE ENGLISH LANGUAGE

| | TITLE | AUTHOR | WORD COUNT |
|---|---|---|---|
| 1 | *Mission Earth* | **L. Ron Hubbard** | **1,200,000 words** |
| 2 | *Sironia, Texas* | Madison Cooper | 1,100,000 words |
| 3 | *Clarissa* | Samuel Richardson | 969,000 words |
| 4 | *Poor Fellow My Country* | Xavier Herbert | 850,000 words |
| 5 | *Miss MacIntosh, My Darling* | Marguerite Young | 700,000 words |
| 6 | *A Suitable Boy* | Vikram Seth | 593,674 words |
| 7 | *Atlas Shrugged* | Ayn Rand | 565,223 words |
| 8 | *Remembrance Rock* | Carl Sandburg | 532,030 words |
| 9 | *Gai-Jin* | James Clavell | 487,700 words |
| 10 | *Infinite Jest* | David Foster Wallace | 484,001 words |

# LITERATURE IN NUMBERS

**The longest non-fiction book** – *The Yongle Dadian* – 10,000 volumes (only 100 survive)

**The most prolific author** – Barbara Cartland – 723 novels in her lifetime

**The longest first print run** – *Harry Potter and the Deathly Hallows* – 12 million copies in 2007

**The longest sentence in a novel** – in Victor Hugo's *Les Misérables*, comprising 823 words, 93 commas, 51 semicolons and four dashes

# THE HARRY POTTER BOOKS

| TITLE | YEAR PUBLISHED | FIRST PRINT RUN IN USA |
| --- | --- | --- |
| *The Philosopher's Stone* | June 1997 | 50,000 copies |
| *The Chamber of Secrets* | July 1998 | 250,000 copies |
| *The Prisoner of Azkaban* | July 1999 | 500,000 copies |
| *The Goblet of Fire* | July 2000 | 3.8 million copies |
| *The Order of the Phoenix* | June 2003 | 6.8 million copies |
| *The Half-Blood Prince* | July 2005 | 10.8 million copies |
| *The Deathly Hallows* | July 2007 | 12 million copies |
| *The Cursed Child** | July 2016 | 4.5 million copies |

\* Play script by Jack Thorne, story by Thorne, J. K. Rowling and John Tiffany

# MUSIC

# TOP TEN BESTSELLING ARTISTS OF ALL TIME

| | ARTIST | NO. OF ALBUMS SOLD |
|---|---|---|
| 1 | **The Beatles** | **Over 265 million** |
| 2 | Elvis Presley | Over 210 million |
| 3 | Rihanna | Over 190 million |
| 4 | Michael Jackson | Over 175 million |
| 5 | Madonna | Over 166 million |
| 6 | Elton John | Over 162 million |
| 7 | Garth Brooks | 145 million |
| 8 | Led Zeppelin | 140 million |
| 9 | The Eagles | Over 130 million |
| 10 | Mariah Carey | 130 million |

# UK MUSIC RECORD SALES CERTIFICATIONS

| DISC | SINGLE SALES | ALBUM SALES |
|---|---|---|
| Silver | 200,000 | 60,000 |
| Gold | 400,000 | 100,000 |
| Platinum | 600,000 | 300,000 |
| Multiplatinum | 1.2 million | 600,000 |

# TOP TEN MOST COVERED SONGS

| | SONG TITLE | ARTIST |
|---|---|---|
| 1 | 'Yesterday' | **The Beatles** |
| 2 | 'Eleanor Rigby' | The Beatles |
| 3 | 'Cry Me a River' | Julie London |
| 4 | 'And I Love Her' | The Beatles |
| 5 | '(I Can't Get No) Satisfaction' | The Rolling Stones |
| 6 | 'Imagine' | John Lennon |
| 7 | 'Summertime' | Abbie Mitchell |
| 8 | 'Blackbird' | The Beatles |
| 9 | 'Over the Rainbow' | Judy Garland |
| 10 | 'The Look of Love' | Dusty Springfield |

# TOP TEN SELLING ARTISTS BY DIGITAL DOWNLOAD*

| | ARTIST | DOWNLOADS |
|---|---|---|
| 1 | **Rihanna** | **100 million** |
| 2 | Taylor Swift | 89.5 million |
| 3 | Katy Perry | 80.5 million |
| 4 | Kanye West | 47.5 million |
| 5 | Lady Gaga | 39.5 million |
| 6 | Justin Bieber | 35 million |
| 7 | Eminem | 34 million |
| 8 | Lil Wayne | 33 million |
| 9 | Flo Rida | 32.5 million |
| 10 | Drake | 29 million |

*As of August 2015

# TOP FIVE LONGEST CONCERT TOURS

| | |
|---|---|
| **1** | **Cher, Living Proof: The Farewell Tour (14 June 2002 to 30 April 2005), 325 shows** |
| 2 | Thirty Seconds to Mars, Into the Wild Tour (19 February 2010 to 9 December 2011), 304 shows |
| 3 | Leonard Cohen, World Tour (11 May 2008 to 11 December 2010), 246 Shows |
| 4 | Bon Jovi, New Jersey Syndicate Tour (30 October 1988 to 17 February 1990), 232 Shows |
| 5 | Aerosmith, Nine Lives Tour (8 May 1997 to 17 July 1999), 204 shows |

# TEN YEARS OF CHRISTMAS NUMBER ONES

| YEAR | SONG TITLE | ARTIST |
|---|---|---|
| 2015 | 'A Bridge Over You' | Lewisham and Greenwich NHS Choir |
| 2014 | 'Something I Need' | Ben Haenow |
| 2013 | 'Skyscraper' | Sam Bailey |
| 2012 | 'He Ain't Heavy, He's My Brother' | The Justice Collective |
| 2011 | 'Wherever You Are' | Military Wives with Gareth Malone |
| 2010 | 'When We Collide' | Matt Cardle |
| 2009 | 'Killing in the Name' | Rage Against the Machine |
| 2008 | 'Hallelujah' | Alexandra Burke |
| 2007 | 'When You Believe' | Leon Jackson |
| 2006 | 'A Moment Like This' | Leona Lewis |

# UK BESTSELLING RECORDS OF THE YEAR (PAST TEN YEARS)

| YEAR | SONG TITLE | ARTIST |
|------|-----------|--------|
| 2015 | 'Uptown Funk' | Mark Ronson feat. Bruno Mars |
| 2014 | 'Happy' | Pharrell Williams |
| 2013 | 'Blurred Lines' | Robin Thicke feat. T. I. and Pharrell Williams |
| 2012 | 'Somebody that I Used to Know' | Gotye feat. Kimbra |
| 2011 | 'Someone Like You' | Adele |
| 2010 | 'Love the Way You Lie' | Eminem feat. Rihanna |
| 2009 | 'Poker Face' | Lady Gaga |
| 2008 | 'Hallelujah' | Alexandra Burke |
| 2007 | 'Bleeding Love' | Leona Lewis |
| 2006 | 'Crazy' | Gnarls Barkley |

# TOP TEN BIGGEST CONCERT ATTENDANCES

| | ARTIST | LOCATION AND DATE | NO. OF TICKETS SOLD |
|---|---|---|---|
| =1 | **Jean-Michel Jarre** | **Moscow (6 September 1997)** | **3,500,000** |
| =1 | **Rod Stewart** | **Copacabana Beach, Rio (31 December 1994)** | **3,500,000** |
| 3 | New York Philharmonic | Central Park, New York (5 July 1986) | 800,000 |
| 4 | Garth Brooks | Central Park, New York (7 August 1997) | 750,000 |
| 5 | Various artists | 1983 USA Festival (28–30 May 1983) | 670,000 |
| 6 | Various artists | Summer Jam at Watkins Glen, New York (28 July 1973) | 600,000+ |
| 7 | Various artists | Isle of Wight Festival (1970) | 600,000 |
| 8 | Simon & Garfunkel | Central Park, New York (19 September 1981) | 500,000 |
| 9 | Various artists, Toronto SARS Benefit (30 July 2003) | 450,000 | |
| 10 | Various artists | Woodstock (1969) | 400,000 |

# TOP TEN LONGEST SONGS

| 1 | 'In the Garden', PC III label Pipe Choir – 181 minutes and 50 seconds |
|---|---|
| 2 | 'Surgical Sound Specimens from the Museum of Skin', Fantômas – 74 minutes and 17 seconds |
| 3 | 'Dopesmoker', Sleep – 63 minutes and 31 seconds |
| 4 | 'The Incident', The Porcupine Tree – 55 minutes and 8 seconds |
| 5 | 'Mountain Jam', Allman Brothers – 44 minutes |
| 6 | 'Georgia on My Mind / In Memory of Elizabeth Reed', Allman Brothers – 43 minutes and 57 seconds |
| 7 | 'Part 10 Exit Music (The Beginning Stages of...)', The Polyphonic Spree – 36 minutes and 30 seconds |
| 8 | 'Performance 2', Jam Fruscante – 35 minutes and 32 seconds |
| 9 | 'Red Flag (The Secret in Disguise)', Sunburned Hand of the Man – 34 minutes and 52 seconds |
| 10 | 'Zone', Lightning Bolt – 32 minutes and 46 seconds |

# TOP TEN MOST SUCCESSFUL CONCERT TOURS (BY ATTENDANCE)

| | ARTIST | LOCATION AND DATE | NO. OF TICKETS SOLD |
|---|---|---|---|
| 1 | **U2** | **360° Tour, U2 (30 June 2009 to 30 July 2011)** | **7,300,000** |
| 2 | The Rolling Stones | Voodoo Lounge Tour (1 August 1994 to 30 August 1995) | 6,300,000 |
| 3 | Pink Floyd | The Division Lounge Tour (30 March 1994 to 29 October 1994) | 6,000,000 |
| 4 | AC/DC | Black Ice World Tour (28 October 2008 to 28 June 2010) | 4,800,000 |
| 5 | The Rolling Stones | A Bigger Bang Tour (21 to 26 August 2007) | 4,680,000 |
| 6 | U2 | Vertigo Tour (28 March to 9 December 2006) | 4,619,021 |
| 7 | Michael Jackson | HIStory World Tour (7 September 1996 to 15 October 1997) | 4,500,000 |
| 8 | Michael Jackson | Bad World Tour (12 September 1987 to 27 January 1989) | 4,400,000 |
| 9 | U2 | PopMart Tour, U2 (25 April 1997 to 21 March 1998) | 3,935,936 |
| 10 | Bruce Springsteen | Wrecking Bull World Tour (18 March 2012 to 21 March 2013) | 3,650,000 |

## MADONNA'S TOP FIVE MOST SUCCESSFUL STUDIO ALBUMS

| | ALBUM TITLE | YEAR OF RELEASE | UNITS SOLD |
|---|---|---|---|
| 1 | *True Blue* | 1986 | 25 million |
| 2 | *Like a Virgin* | 1984 | 21 million |
| 3 | *Ray of Light* | 1998 | 16 million |
| =4 | *Like a Prayer* | 1989 | 15 million |
| =4 | *Music* | 2000 | 15 million |

## THE BEATLES' UK OFFICIAL STUDIO ALBUMS

| | ALBUM TITLE | RELEASE DATE |
|---|---|---|
| 1 | *Please Please Me* | 22 March 1963 |
| 2 | *With the Beatles* | 22 November 1963 |
| 3 | *A Hard Day's Night* | 10 July 1964 |
| 4 | *Beatles for Sale* | 4 December 1964 |
| 5 | *Help!* | 6 August 1965 |
| 6 | *Rubber Soul* | 3 December 1965 |
| 7 | *Revolver* | 5 August 1966 |
| 8 | *Sgt Pepper's Lonely Hearts Club Band* | 1 June 1967 |
| 9 | *The White Album* | 22 November 1968 |
| 10 | *Yellow Submarine* | 13 January 1969 |
| 11 | *Abbey Road* | 26 September 1969 |
| 12 | *Let It Be* | 8 May 1970 |

# WORLD'S BIGGEST RECORD LABELS (BY REVENUE)*

|  | RECORD LABEL | REVENUE |
|---|---|---|
| 1 | **Universal Music Group** | **$5.6 billion** |
| 2 | Sony Music Entertainment | $5.51 billion |
| 3 | Warner Music Group | $2.996 billion |
| 4 | EMI Group | $1.6 billion |

* As of 2015

# TOP FIVE FASTEST RAPPERS

| =1 | **Don Xperto – 25 syllables per second (in Spanish)** |
|---|---|
| =1 | **Crucified – 25 syllables per second** |
| 3 | Rebel XD – 20.29 syllables per second |
| 4 | Outsider – 18.5 syllables per second (in Korean) |
| 5 | NoClue – 17.51 syllables per second |

# TOP TEN MOST EXPENSIVE MUSIC VIDEOS

| | SONG TITLE | ARTIST | PRODUCTION COST |
|---|---|---|---|
| 1 | **'Scream'** | **Michael Jackson and Janet Jackson** | **$7 million** |
| 2 | 'Die Another Day' | Madonna | $6.1 million+ |
| =3 | 'Express Yourself' | Madonna | $5 million+ |
| =3 | 'Bedtime Story' | Madonna | $5 million+ |
| =5 | 'Black or White' | Michael Jackson | $4 million |
| =5 | 'Estranged' | Guns N' Roses | $4 million |
| =5 | 'Make Me Like You' | Gwen Stefani | $4 million |
| 8 | 'Victory' | Puff Daddy (feat. Notorious B.I.G. and Busta Rhymes) | $2.7 million+ |
| =9 | '2 Legit 2 Quit' | MC Hammer | $2.5 million+ |
| =9 | 'Heartbreaker' | Mariah Carey (feat. Jay-Z) | $2.5 million |

# TOP TEN LOUDEST BANDS

| 1 | **Sleazy Joe – 143.2 dB – 2008 in Hässleholm, Sweden** |
|---|---|
| 2 | Swans – 140 dB – 1985 in London |
| 3 | Manowar – 139 dB – 2008 at the Magic Circle Fest |
| 4 | Leftfield – 137 dB – June 1996 in London |
| 5 | KISS – 136 dB – July 2009 at the Cisco Ottawa BluesFest in Ottawa, Canada |
| 6 | Gallows – 132.5 dB – 2007 in a recording studio |
| 7 | My Bloody Valentine – 132 dB |
| =8 | AC/DC – 130 dB – during the 'Back in Black' tour, 1980–81 |
| =8 | Led Zeppelin – 'Heartbreaker' is said to have reached 130 dB |
| =8 | Motörhead – 130 dB – though this claim is unverified |

## Fascinating Fact

- Hearing damage (due to long-term exposure to loud noise) starts around 85 decibels!

# TOP TEN ALL-TIME BESTSELLING ALBUMS IN THE UK

|  | ALBUM | ARTIST | UNITS SOLD |
|---|---|---|---|
| **1** | ***Greatest Hits*** | **Queen** | **6 million** |
| =2 | *Gold: Greatest Hits* | ABBA | 5.1 million |
| =2 | *Sgt Pepper's Lonely Hearts Club Band* | The Beatles | 5.1 million |
| 4 | *21* | Adele | 4.9 million |
| 5 | *(What's the Story) Morning Glory?* | Oasis | 4.6 million |
| 6 | *Brothers in Arms* | Dire Straits | 4.4 million |
| 7 | *Thriller* | Michael Jackson | 4.3 million |
| 8 | *The Dark Side of the Moon* | Pink Floyd | 4.2 million |
| =9 | *Bad* | Michael Jackson | 3.9 million |
| =9 | *Greatest Hits: Volume Two* | Queen | 3.9 million |

# THE ORCHESTRA

The typical symphony orchestra consists of four proportionate groups of similar musical instruments. See examples below:

| SECTION | INSTRUMENTS |
|---|---|
| **Woodwinds** | Piccolo, flute, oboe, English horn, clarinet, bass clarinet, bassoon, contrabassoon |
| **Brass** | French horn, trumpet, trombone, bass trombone, tuba |
| **Percussion** | Timpani, snare drum, bass drum, cymbals, triangle, celesta |
| **Strings** | Harp, violin, viola, cello, double bass |

## Fascinating Facts

- Domenico Dragonetti (1763–1846) was the first great virtuoso of the double bass; he was largely responsible for its permanent place in the orchestra.

- The clarinet's predecessor was the chalumeau, the first true single-reed instrument.

- The name for the dulcimer (a type of zither) comes from the Latin and Greek works *dulce* and *melos*, which combine to mean 'sweet tune'.

- The ocarina, a wind instrument, is also known as the sweet potato, due to its resemblance.

- A piano covers the full spectrum of all orchestra instruments, from below the lowest note of the contrabassoon to above the top note of the piccolo. A grand piano can be played faster than an upright (spinet) piano.

- Guitar probably comes from the word *kithara*, which was the principal stringed instrument of the Ancient Greeks and later of the Romans. The kithara was played with a plectrum and it was a larger and stronger form of the lyre.

# MUSICAL FIRSTS

- In the 1820s, Louis Spohr introduced the conductor's baton.
- The CD was developed by Philips and Sony in 1980.
- The LP (long-playing) record was invented by Paul Goldmark in 1948.
- At the first Grammy Awards, held on 4 May 1959, Domenico Modugno won 'Record of the Year', with 'Volare'.
- The first pop video was 'Bohemian Rhapsody' by Queen, released in 1975.
- In 1987, queen of soul Aretha Franklin was the first female artist to be inducted into the Rock 'n' Roll Hall of Fame, followed by The Supremes in 1988.
- Beethoven was the first composer who never had an official court position, thus the first known freelance musician.
- The first ever number one, when the charts began in 1952, was Al Martino's 'Here in My Heart'.
- In 1473, just a few decades after the invention of the printing press by Johannes Gutenberg, the first mechanically printed music, 'Constance Gradual', was published in southern Germany.

# MUSICAL MOSTS

- Robbie Williams holds the record for the most Brit awards: 12 as a solo artist and another five as part of Take That.
- The harmonica is the world's bestselling musical instrument.
- More than 2,500 cover versions of The Beatles' 'Yesterday' exist, making it the most recorded song in history.
- The British (per capita) spend the most on prerecorded music.

# TOP FIVE BESTSELLING SINGLES OF ALL TIME

| | |
|---|---|
| **1** | **'White Christmas', Bing Crosby – 50 million** |
| 2 | 'Candle in the Wind 1997', Elton John – 33 million |
| =3 | 'Silent Night', Bing Crosby – 30 million |
| =3 | 'In the Summertime', Mungo Jerry – 30 million |
| 5 | 'Rock Around the Clock', Bill Haley – 25 million |

# MOZART'S MILESTONES

**1756** – Born in Salzburg, Austria, on 27 January.

**1762** – Embarked with his father and sister on the first of many concert tours through Europe.

**1769** – Became honorary concertmaster to the archbishop of Salzburg, a position he retained until 1781.

**1770** – Produced the opera *Mithridates, King of Pontus*.

**1770** – Was made a chevalier of the 'Order of the Golden Spur' by Pope Clement XIV.

**1781** – The opera *Idomeneo, King of Crete*, was first performed.

**1781** – Left his post in Salzburg and spent the last years of his life working in Vienna as a composer and teacher.

**1786** – The opera *The Marriage of Figaro* was first performed.

**1787** – The opera *Don Giovanni* was first performed.

**1790** – The opera *Così fan Tutte* was first performed.

**1791** – Composed *The Magic Flute*. Died on 5 December and laid to rest in an unmarked grave.

# MUSICAL INSTRUCTIONS (SPEED)

| INSTRUCTION | MEANING |
| --- | --- |
| Largo | Very slow |
| Lento | Slowly |
| Adagio | Slow |
| Andante | Walking pace |
| Moderato | Moderately |
| Allegro | Quick and lively |
| Molto allegro | Very fast |
| Presto | Very quickly |
| Prestissimo | As fast as possible |
| Rallentando | Slowing down |
| Accelerando | Speeding up |

# MUSICAL INSTRUCTIONS (CHARACTER)

| Con brio | With vigour |
| --- | --- |
| Dolce | Sweetly |
| Doloroso | Sadly |
| Giocoso | Merrily |
| Leggiero | Lightly |
| Pesante | Heavily |
| Maestoso | Majestically |
| Scherzando | Jokingly playfully |
| Vivace | Lively |

**MUSICAL INSTRUCTIONS (SOUND)**

| | |
|---|---|
| Pianissimo | Very soft |
| Piano | Soft |
| Mezzo piano | Medium soft |
| Mezzo forte | Medium loud |
| Forte | Loud |
| Fortissimo | Very loud |
| Diminuendo | Getting softer |
| Crescendo | Getting louder |

 **MUSICAL INSTRUCTIONS (TECHNICAL)**

| | |
|---|---|
| Attacca | Continue without break |
| Da Capo | Return to beginning |
| Arco | Bowed |
| Pizzicato | Plucked |
| Glissando | Slide |
| Legato | Smoothly |
| Staccato | Detached |
| Volta subito | Turn page quickly |
| Fine | End |
| Con | With |
| Senza | Without |
| Molto | Very |
| Poco | A little |

# THE NATURAL WORLD

# TOP TEN WORLD'S LARGEST DESERTS

| | DESERT | LOCATION | SIZE |
|---|---|---|---|
| **1** | **Antarctica** | **South Pole** | **5,500,000 sq miles (14,200,000 sq km)** |
| 2 | Arctic | North Pole | 5,400,000 sq miles (13,900,000 sq km) |
| 3 | Sahara | North Africa | 3,500,000 sq miles (9,000,000 sq km) |
| 4 | Arabian | Egypt | 900,000 sq miles (2,330,000 sq km) |
| 5 | Gobi | Mongolia, China | 500,000 sq miles (1,300,000 sq km) |
| 6 | Kalahari | Bostwana, Namibia, South Africa | 360,000 sq miles (900,000 sq km) |
| 7 | Patagonian | South America | 300,000 sq miles (776,996 sq km) |
| 8 | Taklimakan Shamo | Mongolia, China | 140,000 sq miles (362,000 sq km) |
| 9 | Great Victoria | Australia | 135,000 sq miles (350,000 sq km) |
| 10 | Kara Kum | Turkmenistan | 120,000 sq miles (310,000 sq km) |

# MOST POPULOUS CITIES ON EARTHQUAKE FAULT LINES

| 1 | Tokyo |
|---|-------|
| 2 | Mexico City |
| 3 | New York |
| 4 | Mumbai |
| 5 | Delhi |
| 6 | Shanghai |
| 7 | Kolkata |
| 8 | Jakarta |

# TOP TEN WORLD'S HOTTEST PLACES

| | PLACE | COUNTRY | HIGHEST RECORDED TEMPERATURE |
|---|-------|---------|------------------------------|
| 1 | Death Valley | California, USA | 56.7°C* (134°F) |
| =2 | Ghadames | Libya | 55°C (131°F) |
| =2 | Kebili | Tunisia | 55°C (131°F) |
| 4 | Timbuktu | Mali | 54.5°C (130.1°F) |
| 5 | Araouane | Mali | 54.4°C (130°F) |
| 6 | Tirat Tavi | Israel | 53.8°C (129°F) |
| 7 | Ahwaz | Iran | 53.5°C (128.3°F) |
| 8 | Aghajari | Iran | 53.3°C (128°F) |
| 9 | Wadi Halfa | Sudan | 52.7°C (127°F) |
| 10 | Jeddah | Saudi Arabia | 52°C (125.6°F) |

* Highest temperature in the world reliably recorded. The highest temperature in the world ever recorded was 58°C (136.4°F) in 1922 at Al'Aziziyah, Libya, but the World Meterological Organisation announced in 2012 that the reading was invalid as it could not be verified

# TOP TEN WORLD'S COLDEST PLACES*

| | PLACE | COUNTRY | LOWEST RECORDED TEMPERATURE |
|---|---|---|---|
| **1** | **Vostok Station** | **Antarctica** | **−89.2°C (−128.6°F)** |
| 2 | Plateau Station | Antarctic | −84°C (−119.2°F) |
| 3 | Mount McKinley | Alaska | −73.8°C (−101°F) |
| 4 | Oymyakon | Russia | −71.1°C (−96°F) |
| 5 | Klinck Research Station | Greenland | −69.4°C (−93°F) |
| 6 | Verkhoyansk | Russia | −67.7°C (−90°F) |
| 7 | North Ice | Greenland | −66°C (−87°F) |
| 8 | Eismitte | Greenland | −64.9°C (−85°F) |
| 9 | Snag | Yukon, Canada | −63°C (−81.4°F) |
| 10 | Prospect Creek | Alaska, USA | −62.1°C (−79.8°F) |

* The lowest temperature ever recorded on earth is −93.2°C (−136°F) at Dome Fuji Ridge, East Antarctic Plateau, but this is not counted as a world record because it was recorded by a NASA satellite and not directly recorded in situ

# TOP TEN WORLD'S LONGEST MOUNTAIN RANGES

| | MOUNTAIN RANGE | LOCATION | SIZE |
|---|---|---|---|
| **1** | **Mid-Atlantic Ridge** | **Arctic Ocean to southern tip of Africa** | **10,000 miles (16,000 km)*** |
| 2 | Cordillera de Los Andes | South America | 4,500 miles (7,200 km) |
| 3 | Rocky Mountains | North America | 3,000 miles (4,800 km) |
| 4 | Himalaya–Karakoram–Hindu Kush | Central Asia | 2,400 miles (3,850 km) |
| 5 | Great Dividing Range | Australia | 2,250 miles (3,620 km) |
| 6 | Trans-Antarctic Mountains | Antarctica | 2,200 miles (3,540 km) |
| 7 | Atlantic Coast Range | Brazil | 1,900 miles (3,050 km) |
| 8 | West Sumatran–Javan Range | Indonesia | 1,800 miles (2,900 km) |
| 9 | Aleutian Range | Alaska and north-west Pacific | 1,650 miles (2,650 km) |
| 10 | Tien Shan | Central Asia | 1,400 miles (2,250 km) |

* 90 per cent of this continuous mountain range is underwater

# TOP TEN WORLD'S LARGEST LAKES

| | LAKE | LOCATION | SIZE |
|---|---|---|---|
| **1** | **Caspian Sea** | **Iran/Azerbaijan/ Russia/ Turkmenistan/ Kazakhstan** | **143,000 sq miles (371,000 sq km)** |
| 2 | Michigan–Huron | USA/Canada | 45,300 sq miles (117,610 sq km) |
| 3 | Superior | Canada/USA | 31,700 sq miles (82,100 sq km) |
| 4 | Victoria | Uganda/Tanzania/ Kenya | 26,828 sq miles (69,500 sq km) |
| 5 | Tanganyika | Democratic Republic of the Congo/Tanzania/ Zambia/Burundi | 12,665 sq miles (32,900 sq km) |
| 6 | Great Bear | Canada | 12,096 sq miles (31,328 sq km) |
| 7 | Baykal (Baikal) | Russia | 11,776 sq miles (30,500 sq km) |
| 8 | Malawi (Nyasa) | Tanzania/Malwai/ Mozambique | 11,150 sq miles (28,900 sq km) |
| 9 | Great Slave | Canada | 11,031 sq miles (28,570 sq km) |
| 10 | Erie | Canada/USA | 9,910 sq miles (25,670 sq km) |

# TOP TEN WORLD'S DEEPEST LAKES

| | LAKE | LOCATION | SIZE |
|---|---|---|---|
| **1** | **Baikal** | **Russia** | **1,637 m (5,371 ft)** |
| 2 | Tanganyika | Burundi/Tanzania/ Democratic Republic of the Congo/Zambia | 1,470 m (4,825 ft) |
| 3 | Caspian Sea | Azerbaijan/Iran/ Kazakhstan/Russia/ Turkmenistan | 1,025 m (3,363 ft)* |
| 4 | Vostok | Antarctica | 900 m (2,953 ft) |
| 5 | O'Higgins/ San Martín | Chile/Argentina | 836 m (2,742 ft) |
| 6 | Malawi | Malawi/ Mozambique/ Tanzania | 706 m (2,316 ft) |
| 7 | Issyk-Kul | Kyrgyzstan | 702 m (2,303 ft) |
| 8 | Great Slave | Canada | 614 m (2,015 ft) |
| 9 | Crater Lake | Oregon, USA | 594 m (1,949 ft) |
| 10 | Matano (Matana) | Indonesia | 590 m (1,936 ft) |

* Also world's third deepest sea

# TEN OF THE WORLD'S BIGGEST RECORDED EARTHQUAKES

| | PLACE | DATE | RICHTER MAGNITUDE |
|---|---|---|---|
| 1 | **Chile (offshore)** | **22 May 1960** | **9.5** |
| 2 | Prince William Sound, Alaska | 28 March 1964 | 9.2 |
| 3 | Northern Sumatra (offshore), Indonesia | 26 December 2004 | 9.1 |
| =4 | Tohoku, Japan | 11 March 2011 | 9.0 |
| =4 | Kamchatka, Russia | 4 November 1952 | 9.0 |
| =6 | Chile (offshore) | 27 February 2010 | 8.8 |
| =6 | Ecuador (offshore) | 31 January 1906 | 8.8 |
| 8 | Rat Islands, Alaska | 4 February 1965 | 8.7 |
| 9 | Northern Sumatra (offshore), Indonesia | 28 March 2005 | 8.6 |
| 10 | Assam, Tibet | 15 August 1950 | 8.6 |

# TEN OF THE WORLD'S DEADLIEST EARTHQUAKES

| | PLACE | DATE | NUMBER OF FATALITIES |
|---|---|---|---|
| 1 | **Shaanxi Province, China** | **23 January 1556** | **830,000** |
| 2 | Haiti | 12 January 2010 | 316,000 |
| 3 | Tangshan, China | 28 July 1976 | 242,000 |
| 4 | Aleppo, Syria | 9 August 1138 | 230,000 |
| 5 | Sumatra, Indonesia | 26 December 2004 | 227,898 |
| =6 | Gansu, China | 16 December 1920 | 200,000 |
| =6 | Damghan, Iran | 22 December AD 856 | 200,000 |
| 8 | Ardabil, Iran | 23 March AD 893 | 150,000 |
| 9 | Kwanto, Japan | 1 September 1923 | 143,000 |
| 10 | Ashgabat, Turkmenistan | 5 October 1948 | 110,000 |

# TOP TEN HIGHEST ACTIVE VOLCANOES

| | VOLCANO | COUNTRY | HEIGHT ABOVE SEA LEVEL |
|---|---|---|---|
| 1 | **Ojos del Salado** | **Argentina/Chile** | **6,887 m (22,595 ft)** |
| 2 | Llullaillaco | Argentina/Chile | 6,739 m (22,109 ft) |
| 3 | Cerro Tipas | Argentina | 6,660 m (21,850 ft) |
| 4 | Cerro El Cóndor | Argentina | 6,532 m (21,430 ft) |
| 5 | Coropuna | Peru | 6,377 m (20,922 ft) |
| 6 | Parinacota | Chile | 6,348 m, (20,827 ft) |
| 7 | Chimborazo | Ecuador | 6,310 m (20,702 ft) |
| 8 | Pula | Chile | 6,233 m (20,449 ft) |
| 9 | Aucanquilcha | Chile | 6,176m (20,262 ft) |
| 10 | San Pedro | Chile | 6,145 m (20,161 ft) |

# TEN OF THE WORLD'S DEADLIEST VOLCANO ERUPTIONS

| | PLACE | DATE | APPROX. NUMBER OF FATALITIES |
|---|---|---|---|
| 1 | **Tambora, Indonesia** | **1815** | **92,000** |
| 2 | Krakatoa, Indonesia | 1883 | 37,000 |
| 3 | Mount Pelee, Martinique | 1902 | 30,000 |
| 4 | Nevado Del Ruiz, Colombia | 1985 | 23,000 |
| 5 | Mount Vesuvius, Pompeii | AD 79 | 16,000 |
| 6 | Unzen, Japan | 1792 | 14,500 |
| 7 | Kelut, Java | 1586 | 10,100 |
| 8 | Laki, Iceland | 1783* | 10,000 |
| 9 | Kelut, Java | 1919 | 5,000 |
| 10 | Papandayan, Java | 1772 | 3,000 |

* With the eruption from Laki, great clouds of volcanic gasses were released covering much of northern Europe and were probably responsible for many more thousands of deaths

# TEN OF THE WORLD'S MOST DESTRUCTIVE HURRICANES

| | NAME | PLACE | DATE | APPROX. NUMBER OF FATALITIES |
|---|---|---|---|---|
| **1** | **Bhola Cyclone** | **Bangladesh** | **13 November 1970** | **300,000– 500,000** |
| =2 | Calcutta Cyclone | Bengal, India | 7 October 1737 | 300,000 |
| =2 | Haiphong Cyclone | Haiphong, Vietnam | 8 October 1881 | 300,000 |
| 4 | Super Typhoon Nina | China | 7 August 1975 | 210,000 |
| 5 | Bengal Cyclone | Bengal, India | 31 October 1876 | 200,000 |
| 6 | Cyclone Nargis | Burma | 3 May 2008 | 146,000 |
| 7 | Bangladesh Cyclone | Bangladesh | 29 April 1991 | 138,800 |
| 8 | Bombay Cyclone | Bombay, India | 6 June 1882 | 100,000 |
| 9 | Calcutta Cyclone | Calcutta, India | 5 October 1864 | 50,000–70,000 |
| 10 | Swatow Typhoon | China | 1 August 1922 | 60,000 |

# TEN OF THE WORLD'S DEADLIEST FLOODS

| | PLACE | DATE | APPROX. NUMBER OF FATALITIES |
|---|---|---|---|
| 1 | **Huang He (Yellow) River, China** | **1931** | **1,000,000–3,700,000** |
| 2 | Huang He River | 1887 | 900,000–2,000,000 |
| 3 | Huang He River | 1938 | 500,000–900,000 |
| 4 | Kaifeng Flood, China | 1642 | 300,000 |
| 5 | Ru River, Banqiao Dam, China | 1975 | 230,000 |
| 6 | Yangtze River, China | 1931 | 145,000 |
| 7 | The Netherlands and England | 1099 | 100,000 |
| 8 | The Netherlands | 1287 | 50,000–80,000 |
| 9 | Eastern Guatemala | 1949 | 40,000 |
| 10 | Bangladesh monsoon | 1974 | 30,000 |

 # TOP TEN WORLD'S LARGEST SEAS

| | SEA | SIZE |
|---|---|---|
| 1 | **South China** | **1,148,500 sq miles (2,974,600 sq km)** |
| 2 | Caribbean | 971,400 sq miles (2,515,900 sq km) |
| 3 | Mediterranean | 969,100 sq miles (2,509,900 sq km) |
| 4 | Bering | 873,000 sq miles (2,261,000 sq km) |
| 5 | Gulf of Mexico | 582,100 sq miles (1,507,600 sq km) |
| 6 | Okhotsk | 537,500 sq miles (1,392,000 sq km) |
| 7 | Japan | 391,100 sq miles (1,012,900 sq km) |
| 8 | Hudson Bay | 281,900 sq miles (730,100 sq km) |
| 9 | East China | 256,600 sq miles (664,600 sq km) |
| 10 | Andaman | 218,100 sq miles (564,880 sq km) |

# TOP TEN WORLD'S DEEPEST SEAS

|  | SEA | DEPTH |
|---|---|---|
| 1 | **Caribbean** | **8,605 m (28,232 ft)** |
| 2 | East China | 7,507 m (24,529 ft) |
| 3 | South China | 7,258 m (23,312 ft) |
| 4 | Mediterranean | 5,150 m (16,896 ft) |
| 5 | Andaman | 4,267 m (14,000 ft) |
| 6 | Bering | 3,936 m (12,913 ft) |
| 7 | Gulf of Mexico | 3,504 m (11,496 ft) |
| 8 | Okhotsk | 3,365 m (11,040 ft) |
| 9 | Japan | 3,053 m (10,016 ft) |
| 10 | Red Sea | 2,266 m (7,434 ft) |

# THE WORLD'S OCEANS (BY SIZE)

|  | OCEAN | SIZE |
|---|---|---|
| 1 | **Pacific** | **59,270,000 sq miles (153,557,000 sq km)** |
| 2 | Atlantic | 29,638,000 sq miles (76,762,000 sq km) |
| 3 | Indian | 26,467,000 sq miles (68,556,000 sq km) |
| 4 | Southern | 7,848,300 sq miles (20,327,000 sq km) |
| 5 | Arctic | 5,427,000 sq miles (14,056,000 sq km) |

# TOP TEN WORLD'S LONGEST CAVES

| | CAVE | LENGTH |
|---|---|---|
| 1 | **Mammoth Cave, USA** | **367 miles (590.6 km)** |
| 2 | Jewel Cave, USA | 140 miles (225.4 km) |
| 3 | Optimisticheskaya, Ukraine | 133 miles (215 km) |
| 4 | Wind Cave, USA | 128 miles (205.6 km) |
| 5 | Lechuguilla Cave, USA | 123 miles (198.6 km) |
| 6 | Hölloch, Switzerland | 121 miles (194.2 km) |
| 7 | Fisher Ridge System, USA | 110 miles (177.3 km) |
| 8 | Sistema Ox Bel Ha (submerged), Mexico | 106 miles (169.9 km) |
| 9 | Sistema Sac Actun (submerged), Mexico | 98 miles (157.3 km) |
| 10 | Siebenhengste-Hohgant-Höhle, Switzerland | 96 miles (154 km) |

# TOP TEN DEEPEST DEPRESSIONS ON THE EARTH'S SURFACE

| | PLACE | COUNTRY | DEPTH* |
|---|---|---|---|
| 1 | **The Dead Sea** | **Jordan, Israel** | **408 m (1,338 ft)** |
| 2 | Lake Assal | The Republic of Djibouti | 156 m (511 ft) |
| 3 | Turfan Depression | Xinjiang, China | 153 m (505 ft) |
| 4 | Qattara Depression | Egypt | 132 m (436 ft) |
| 5 | Karagiye Depression | Kazakhstan | 131 m (433 ft) |
| 6 | Danakil Depression | Ethiopia | 125 m (410 ft) |
| 7 | San Julian's Great Depression | Argentina | 105 m (344 ft) |
| 8 | Death Valley | California, USA | 86 m (282 ft) |
| 9 | Salton Sink | California, USA | 71 m (235 ft) |
| 10 | Ustyurt Plateau | Kazakhstan | 70 m (230 ft) |

* Figures indicate the maximum depth below sea level

# TOP TEN WORLD'S LONGEST RIVERS

| 1 | **Nile – Ethiopia, Sudan, Egypt, Uganda, Democratic Republic of the Congo – 4,160 miles (6,695 km)** |
|---|---|
| 2 | Amazon – Peru, Colombia, Brazil, Bolivia, Venezuela, Ecuador, Guyana – 3,969 miles (6,387 km) |
| 3 | Yangtze (Cháng Jiāng) – China – 3,960 miles (6,380 km) |
| 4 | Mississippi – USA – 3,896 miles (6,275 km) |
| 5 | Yenesei – Russia, Mongolia – 3,439 miles (5,536 km) |
| 6 | Huang He – China 3,395– miles (5,464 km) |
| 7 | Ob-Irtysh – Russia – 3,362 miles (5,410 km) |
| 8 | Amur – Russia, China – 2,714 miles (4,368 km) |
| 9 | Congo – Democratic Republic of the Congo, Angola, Zambia, Tanzania, Burundi, Rwanda – 2,716 miles (4,371 km) |
| 10 | Lena – Russia – 2,647 miles (4,260 km) |

# THE LONGEST RIVER IN...

**Australia:** Murray–Darling – 2,330 miles (3,750 km)

**Europe:** Danube – 1,771 miles (2,850 km)

**France:** Loire – 629 miles (1,012 km)

**UK:** Severn – 220 miles (354 km)

**England:** Thames – 215 miles (346 km)

**Scotland:** Tay – 120 miles (193 km)

**Wales:** Towy – 67 miles (108 km)

# TOP TEN WORLD'S HIGHEST MOUNTAINS

|    | MOUNTAIN | LOCATION | HEIGHT |
|----|----------|----------|--------|
| 1  | **Mount Everest** | **Nepal/Tibet** | **8,848 m (29,029 ft)** |
| 2  | K2 | Pakistan/Sinkiang | 8,611 m (28,251 ft) |
| 3  | Kangchenjunga | Nepal/India | 8,586 m (28,169 ft) |
| 4  | Lhotse | Nepal/Tibet | 8,516 m (27,940 ft) |
| 5  | Makalu | Nepal/Tibet | 8,485 m (27,838 ft) |
| 6  | Cho Oyu | Nepal/Tibet | 8,188 m (26,864 ft) |
| 7  | Dhaulagiri | Nepal | 8,167 m (26,795 ft) |
| 8  | Manaslu | Nepal | 8,163 m (26,781 ft) |
| 9  | Nanga Parbat | Pakistan | 8,125 m (26,657 ft) |
| 10 | Annapurna | Nepal | 8,091 m (26,545 ft) |

# THE HIGHEST MOUNTAIN IN...

**South America:** Aconcagua, Argentina – 6,962 m (22,841 ft)

**North America:** Mount McKinley, Alaska – 6,197 m (4,255 ft)

**Africa:** Kilimanjaro, Tanzania – 5,895 m (19,341 ft)

**Europe:** Mount Elbrus, Russia – 5,642 m (18,510 ft)

**Australia:** Mount Kosciuszko, New South Wales – 2,228 m (7,310 ft)

**Scotland:** Ben Nevis Lochaber – 1,344 m (4,409 ft)

**Ireland:** Carrauntoohil, Kerry – 1,038 m (3,406 ft)

**Wales:** Snowdon, Snowdonia – 1,038 m (3,406 ft)

**England:** Scafell Pike, Cumbria – 978 m (3,209 ft)

# TOP FIVE LARGEST ISLANDS

| 1 | **Greenland** |
|---|---|
| 2 | New Guinea |
| 3 | Borneo |
| 4 | Madagascar |
| 5 | Baffin Island |

# TOP TEN WORLD'S TALLEST WATERFALLS

| | WATERFALL | COUNTRY | HEIGHT |
|---|---|---|---|
| 1 | **Angel Falls** | **Venezuela** | **979 m (3,212 ft)** |
| 2 | Tugela Falls | South Africa | 948 m (3,110 ft) |
| 3 | Three Sisters | Peru | 914 m (3,000 ft) |
| 4 | Olo'upena | Hawaii, USA | 900 m (2,953 ft) |
| 5 | Yumbilla | Amazonas, Peru | 896 m (2,938 ft) |
| 6 | Vinnufallet | Norway | 865 m (2,837 ft) |
| 7 | Skorga | Norway | 864 m (2,835 ft) |
| =8 | Pu'uka'oku Falls | Hawaii, USA | 840 m (2,756 ft) |
| =8 | James Bruce Falls | British Columbia, Canada | 840 m (2,756 ft) |
| 10 | Browne Falls | South Island, New Zealand | 836 m (2,744 ft) |

# TOP TEN WORLD'S MOST POLLUTED CITIES*

|   | CITY | COUNTRY | CAUSE |
|---|------|---------|-------|
| 1 | **Zabol** | **Iran** | **Climate change, dust storms and pollution** |
| 2 | Gwalior | India | Automobile emissions |
| 3 | Allahabad | India | Automobile emissions |
| 4 | Riyadh | Saudi Arabia | Automobile and industrial emissions |
| 5 | Al Jubail | Saudi Arabia | Industrial emissions |
| 6 | Patna | India | Automobile emissions |
| 7 | Raipur | India | Industrial emissions |
| 8 | Bamenda | Cameroon | Industrial emissions |
| 9 | Xingtai | China | Industrial emissions |
| 10 | Baoding | China | Automobile and industrial emissions |

* According to World Health Organisation figures on air pollution

# THE WORLD'S CONTINENTS (BY SIZE)

| CONTINENT | SIZE |
|-----------|------|
| **Asia** | **17,212,048 sq miles (44,579,000 sq km)** |
| Africa | 11,608,161 sq miles (30,065,000 sq km) |
| North America | 9,365,294 sq miles (24,256,000 sq km) |
| South America | 6,879,954 sq miles (17,819,000 sq km) |
| Antarctica | 5,100,023 sq miles (13,209,000 sq km) |
| Europe | 3,837,083 sq miles (9,938,000 sq km) |
| Australia/Oceania | 2,967,967 sq miles (7,687,000 sq km) |

# CONTINENTS (BY POPULATION)*

| | | |
|---|---|---|
| **1** | **Asia – 4,343,450,503** | |
| 2 | Africa – 1,156,434,405 | |
| 3 | Europe – 745,615,793 | |
| 4 | North America – 356,602,286 | |
| 5 | Latin America – 617,243,759 | |
| 6 | Australia/Oceania – 37,143,264 | |
| 7 | Antarctica – 0** | |

\* As of 2015
\*\* Antarctica has no indigenous population, but it does have a fluctuating population based at research stations

# TOP TEN HIGHEST CITIES IN THE WORLD

| | CITY | COUNTRY | HEIGHT |
|---|---|---|---|
| **1** | **La Rinconada** | **Peru** | **5,100 m (16,728 ft)** |
| 2 | El Alto | Bolivia | 4,150 m (13,615 ft) |
| 3 | Potosí | Bolivia | 4,090 m (13,420 ft) |
| 4 | Laya | Bhutan | 3,850 m (12,631 ft) |
| 5 | Shigatse | Tibet | 3,840 m (12,600 ft) |
| 6 | Juliaca | Peru | 3,825 m (12,549 ft) |
| 7 | Oruro | Bolivia | 3,709 m (12,159 ft) |
| 8 | Lhasa | Tibet | 3,650 m (11,975 ft) |
| 9 | Cuzco | Peru | 3,310 m (10,800 ft) |
| 10 | Leadville | USA | 3,094 m (10,152 ft) |

# TOP TEN COUNTRIES WITH THE LONGEST COASTLINES

|  | COUNTRY | LENGTH OF COASTLINE |
|---|---|---|
| 1 | **Canada** | **125,567 miles (202,080 km)** |
| 2 | Indonesia | 33,999 miles (54,716 km) |
| 3 | Greenland | 27,394 miles (44,087 km) |
| 4 | Russia | 23,396 miles (37,652 km) |
| 5 | Philippines | 22,559 miles (36,305 km) |
| 6 | Japan | 18,486 miles (29,750 km) |
| 7 | Australia | 16,007 miles (25,760 km) |
| 8 | Norway | 15,626 miles (25,147 km) |
| 9 | USA | 12,380 miles (19,923 km) |
| 10 | New Zealand | 9,404 miles (15,134 km) |

## Fascinating Fact

- The world has an amazing 221,208 miles (356,000 km) of coastline.

# TOP TEN MAJOR-IMPACT CRATERS ON EARTH (BY DIAMETER)

| | CRATER | COUNTRY | DIAMETER |
|---|---|---|---|
| 1 | **Vredefort** | **South Africa** | **185 miles (300 km)** |
| 2 | Chicxulub | Mexico | 93 miles (150 km) |
| 3 | Sudbury Basin | Canada | 81 miles (130 km) |
| =4 | Popigai | Russia | 62 miles (100 km) |
| =4 | Manicouagan | Canada | 62 miles (100 km) |
| 6 | Acraman | Australia | 56 miles (90 km) |
| 7 | Chesapeake Bay | USA | 53 miles (85 km) |
| 8 | Morokweng | South Africa | 44 miles (70 km) |
| 9 | Kara | Russia | 40 miles (65 km) |
| 10 | Beaverhead | USA | 37 miles (60 km) |

# PLACES

# MOTTOS OF THE 50 STATES OF AMERICA*

| STATE | MOTTO |
| --- | --- |
| Alabama | We Dare Defend Our Rights |
| Alaska | North to the Future |
| Arizona | God Enriches |
| Arkansas | The People Rule |
| California | I Have Found It |
| Colorado | Nothing Without Providence |
| Connecticut | He Who Transplanted Sustains |
| Delaware | Liberty and Independence |
| Florida | In God We Trust |
| Georgia | Wisdom, Justice, and Moderation |
| Hawaii | The Life of the Land is Perpetuated in Righteousness |
| Idaho | Let It Be Perpetual |
| Illinois | State Sovereignty, National Union |
| Indiana | The Crossroads of America |
| Iowa | Our Liberties We Prize and Our Rights We Will Maintain |
| Kansas | To the Stars Through Difficulties |
| Kentucky | United We Stand, Divided We Fall |
| Louisiana | Union, Justice, and Confidence |
| Maine | I Lead |
| Maryland | Manly Deeds, Womanly Words |
| Massachusetts | By the Sword We Seek Peace, But Peace Only Under Liberty |
| Michigan | If You Seek a Pleasant Peninsula, Look About You |
| Minnesota | The Star of the North |
| Mississippi | By Valor and Arms |

| STATE | MOTTO |
| --- | --- |
| Missouri | Let the Welfare of the People Be the Supreme Law |
| Montana | Gold and Silver |
| Nebraska | Equality Before the Law |
| Nevada | All For Our Country |
| New Hampshire | Live Free or Die |
| New Jersey | Liberty and Prosperity |
| New Mexico | It Grows as It Goes |
| New York | Ever Upward |
| North Carolina | To Be, Rather Than to Seem |
| North Dakota | Liberty and Union, Now and Forever, One and Inseparable |
| Ohio | With God, All Things Are Possible |
| Oklahoma | Labor Conquers All Things |
| Oregon | She Flies With Her Own Wings |
| Pennsylvania | Virtue, Liberty, and Independence |
| Rhode Island | Hope |
| South Carolina | While I Breathe, I Hope / Ready in Soul and Resource |
| South Dakota | Under God the People Rule |
| Tennessee | Agriculture and Commerce |
| Texas | Friendship |
| Utah | Industry |
| Vermont | Freedom and Unity |
| Virginia | Thus Always to Tyrants |
| Washington | By and By |
| West Virginia | Mountaineers Are Always Free |
| Wisconsin | Forward |
| Wyoming | Equal Rights |

* Mottos in other languages have been translated into English

## Fascinating Facts

- In Alabama, it is illegal to sell peanuts in Lee County after sundown on a Wednesday, and putting salt on a railroad track may be punishable by death.

- In Louisiana, persons could land in jail for up to ten years for stealing an alligator.

- It is illegal to hunt camels in Arizona.

- It is illegal to sell one's own eye in the state of Texas. It is also illegal to shoot a buffalo from the second storey of a hotel.

# TOP TEN WORLD'S MOST POPULOUS NATIONS

| | COUNTRY | POPULATION* |
|---|---|---|
| 1 | **China** | **1,376 million** |
| 2 | India | 1,251 million |
| 3 | USA | 321 million |
| 4 | Indonesia | 256 million |
| 5 | Brazil | 204 million |
| 6 | Pakistan | 199 million |
| 7 | Nigeria | 181 million |
| 8 | Bangladesh | 169 million |
| 9 | Russia | 142 million |
| 10 | Japan | 127 million |

* As of November 2015

# TOP TEN WORLD'S LONGEST PLACE NAMES

| | |
|---|---|
| **1** | **Krung thep mahanakhon bovorn ratanakosin mahintharayutthaya mahadilok pop noparatratchathani burirom udomratchanivetmahasathan amornpiman avatarnsathit sakkathattiyavisnukarmprasit – Bangkok, Thailand – 167 letters** |
| 2 | Taumatawhakatangihangakoauauotamateaturipukakapi-kimaungahoronukupokaiwhenuakitanatahu – Hawke's Bay Region, New Zealand – 85 letters* |
| 3 | Gorsafawddachaidraigddanheddogleddollônpenrhynareur-draethceredigion – Gwynedd, North Wales – 67 letters |
| 4 | Llanfairpwllgwyngyllgogerychwyrndrobwllllantysiliogogogoch – Gwynedd, North Wales – 58 letters |
| 5 | El Pueblo de Nuestra Señora la Reina de los Ángeles de la Porciúncula – Los Angeles, California – 57 letters |
| 6 | Chargoggagoggmanchaugagoggchaubunagungamaug – Massachusetts, USA – 43 letters |
| =7 | Lower North Branch Little Southwest Miramichi – a short river in New Brunswick, Canada – 40 letters |
| =7 | Villa Real de la Santa Fé de San Francisco de Asis – Santa Fe, New Mexico – 40 letters |
| 9 | Te Whakatakanga-o-te-ngarehu-o-te-ahi-a-Tamatea – New Zealand – 38 letters |
| 10 | Meallan Liath Coire Mhic Dhubhghaill – Aultanrynie, Highlands, Scotland – 32 letters |

* Translation: The place where Tamatea, the man with the big knees, who slid, climbed and swallowed mountains, known as Land-eater, played on the flute to his loved one

# TOP TEN WORLD'S LARGEST COUNTRIES (BY LAND MASS)

|   | COUNTRY | SIZE |
|---|---------|------|
| 1 | **Russia** | **6,592,846 sq miles (17,075,400 sq km)** |
| 2 | Canada | 3,602,707 sq miles (9,330,970 sq km) |
| 3 | China | 3,600,947 sq miles (9,326,410 sq km) |
| 4 | USA | 3,539,242 sq miles (9,166,600 sq km) |
| 5 | Brazil | 3,265,075 sq miles (8,456,510 sq km) |
| 6 | Australia | 2,941,283 sq miles (7,617,930 sq km) |
| 7 | India | 1,147,949 sq miles (2,973,190 sq km) |
| 8 | Argentina | 1,056,636 sq miles (2,736,690 sq km) |
| 9 | Kazakhstan | 1,049,150 sq miles (2,717,300 sq km) |
| 10 | Algeria | 919,595 sq miles (2,381,740 sq km) |

# TOP TEN WORLD'S SMALLEST COUNTRIES

|   | COUNTRY | SIZE |
|---|---------|------|
| 1 | **Vatican City** | **0.17 sq miles (0.44 sq km)** |
| 2 | Monaco | 0.75 sq miles (1.95 sq km) |
| 3 | Nauru | 8.2 sq miles (21.2 sq km) |
| 4 | Tuvalu | 10 sq miles (26 sq km) |
| 5 | San Marino | 24 sq miles (61 sq km) |
| 6 | Liechtenstein | 62 sq miles (160 sq km) |
| 7 | Marshall Islands | 70 sq miles (181 sq km) |
| 8 | Saint Kitts and Nevis | 104 sq miles (261 sq km) |
| 9 | Maldives | 116 sq miles (300 sq km) |
| 10 | Malta | 122 sq miles (316 sq km) |

# COUNTRIES WITH THE MOST LAND BORDERS

| COUNTRY | NO. OF BORDERS |
| --- | --- |
| China | 14 |
| Russian Federation | 14 |
| Brazil | 10 |
| Congo | 9 |
| Germany | 9 |
| Austria | 8 |
| France | 8 |
| Serbia | 8 |
| Tanzania | 8 |
| Turkey | 8 |
| Zambia | 8 |

 # TOP TEN WORLD'S MOST POPULOUS CITIES*

| | CITY | COUNTRY | POPULATION |
| --- | --- | --- | --- |
| 1 | Greater Tokyo | Japan | 37,843,000 |
| 2 | Jakarta (Jabodetabek) | Indonesia | 30,539,000 |
| 3 | Delhi | India | 24,998,000 |
| 4 | Manila | Philippines | 24,123,000 |
| 5 | Seoul | South Korea | 23,480,000 |
| 6 | Shanghai | China | 23,416,000 |
| 7 | Karachi | Pakistan | 22,123,000 |
| 8 | Beijing | China | 21,009,000 |
| 9 | New York City | USA | 20,630,000 |
| 10 | Guangzhou–Foshan | China | 20,597,000 |

\* As of March 2016. Numbers shown include population within the recognised metropolitan area of the city and immediate surroundings

# CITIES AND THEIR RIVERS IN THE UK

| TOWN | RIVER |
| --- | --- |
| Bristol | Avon |
| Canterbury | Stour |
| Cardiff | Taff |
| Carlisle | Eden |
| Colchester | Colne |
| Derby | Derwent |
| Dublin | Liffey |
| Durham | Wear |
| Exeter | Exe |
| Glasgow | Clyde |
| Gloucester | Severn |
| Hereford | Wye |
| Hull | Humber |
| Ipswich | Orwell |
| Lancaster | Lune |
| Leeds | Aire |
| Leicester | Soar |
| Limerick | Shannon |
| Lincoln | Witham |
| Liverpool | Mersey |
| London | Thames |
| Maidstone | Medway |
| Manchester | Irwell |
| Newcastle | Tyne |
| Norwich | Wensum |
| Nottingham | Trent |
| Peterborough | Nene |
| Ripon | Ure |
| Swansea | Tawe |
| York | Ouse |

# COUNTRY CODES FOR CARS

| CODE | COUNTRY |
|------|---------|
| A | Austria |
| AUS | Australia |
| B | Belgium |
| BG | Bulgaria |
| C | Cuba |
| CDN | Canada |
| CH | Switzerland |
| CZ | Czech Republic |
| D | Germany |
| DK | Denmark |
| DZ | Algeria |
| E | Spain |
| EAK | Kenya |
| EST | Estonia |
| F | France |
| FIN | Finland |
| GB | Great Britain |
| GBA | Alderney |
| GBJ | Jersey |
| GBM | Isle of Man |
| GBZ | Gibraltar |
| GDG | Guernsey |
| GR | Greece |
| H | Hungary |
| HKZ | Jordan |
| HR | Croatia |
| I | Italy |
| IL | Israel |

| CODE | COUNTRY |
|------|---------|
| IRL | Ireland |
| J | Japan |
| JA | Jamaica |
| LT | Lithuania |
| LV | Latvia |
| MA | Morocco |
| MC | Monaco |
| N | Norway |
| NL | The Netherlands |
| NZ | New Zealand |
| P | Portugal |
| PE | Peru |
| PL | Poland |
| RA | Argentina |
| RC | China |
| RO | Romania |
| RUS | Russia |
| S | Sweden |
| SLO | Slovenia |
| ZA | South Africa |

# HIGHEST-CIRCULATION NEWSPAPERS IN EUROPE

| NEWSPAPER | COUNTRY |
| --- | --- |
| *ABC* | Spain |
| *Bild* | Germany |
| *Correio da Manhã* | Portugal |
| *Corriere della Sera* | Italy |
| *La Croix* | France |
| *Irish Independent* | Ireland |
| *Kathimerini* | Greece |
| *Het Laatste Nieuws* | Belgium |
| *Morgenavisen Jyllands-Posten* | Denmark |
| *The Sun* | UK |
| *De Telegraaf* | The Netherlands |

# POLITICS

# PARLIAMENTS AROUND THE WORLD

| COUNTRY | PARLIAMENT |
| --- | --- |
| Denmark | Folketing |
| France | Assemblée Nationale |
| Germany | Bundestag and Bundesrat |
| Iceland | Althing |
| India | Lok Sabha and Rajya Sabha |
| Isle of Man | Tynwald |
| Israel | Knesset |
| Italy | Senato |
| Japan | Diet |
| The Netherlands | States-General |
| Norway | Storting |
| Portugal | Cortes |
| Republic of Ireland | Dáil |
| Russia | Duma |
| Spain | Cortes |
| Sweden | Riksdag |
| USA | Congress |

**POLITICAL SYSTEMS AROUND THE WORLD**

| COUNTRY | POLITICAL SYSTEM |
|---|---|
| Australia | Parliamentary monarchy |
| Brazil | Presidential republic |
| Canada | Parliamentary monarchy |
| France | Semi-presidential republic |
| India | Parliamentary republic |
| Iran | Presidential republic under theocratic tutelage |
| Ireland | Parliamentary republic |
| Japan | Parliamentary monarchy |
| Russia | Semi-presidential republic |
| Saudi Arabia | Absolute monarchy |
| Spain | Parliamentary monarchy |
| Thailand | Constitutional monarchy under military junta |
| UK | Parliamentary monarchy |
| USA | Presidential republic |

# COUNTRIES WITH TWO OR MORE CAPITAL CITIES*

| COUNTRY | OFFICIAL CAPITAL | OTHER CAPITAL(S) |
| --- | --- | --- |
| Benin | Porto Novo | Cotonou (de facto seat of government) |
| Bolivia | Sucre (seat of national judiciary) | La Paz (seat of national administrative and legislative bodies) |
| Chile | Santiago (seat of national administrative and judicial bodies) | Valparaís (seat of national legislature) |
| Côte d'Ivoire | Yamoussoukro | Abidjan (de facto seat of government) |
| Malaysia | Kuala Lumpur (seat of national legislature) | Putrajaya (administrative centre and seat of national judiciary) |
| Montenegro | Podgorica | Cetinje ('old royal capital' – historical capital possessing no national governmental functions) |
| The Netherlands | Amsterdam | The Hague (seat of government, i.e. seat of national administrative, legislative, judicial and royal bodies) |
| Philippines | Manila (seat of executive and judiciary) | Pasay City (seat of upper legislature), Quezon City (seat of lower legislature), Baguio City (summer capital, and seat of executive and judiciary during summer months) |

| COUNTRY | OFFICIAL CAPITAL | OTHER CAPITAL(S) |
| --- | --- | --- |
| South Africa | No official capital | Cape Town (legislative capital), Bloemfontein (judicial capital), Pretoria (administrative capital) |
| Sri Lanka | No official capital | Sri Jayawardenepura Kotte (administrative capital), Colombo (commercial capital) |
| Swaziland | No official capital | Mbabane (administrative capital), Lobamba (legislative and royal capital) |
| Tanzania | Dodoma | Dar es Salaam (de facto seat of government) |

* The capital city is the principal city associated with the country's government. Sometimes the official capital is not necessarily the seat of government

# PRIME MINISTERS OF BRITAIN SINCE 1900

| PRIME MINISTER | PARTY | TERM IN OFFICE |
| --- | --- | --- |
| Marquess of Salisbury | Conservative | 1895–1902 |
| Arthur Balfour | Conservative | 1902–5 |
| Sir Henry Campbell-Bannerman | Liberal | 1905–8 |
| Herbert Henry Asquith | Liberal | 1908–16 |
| David Lloyd George | Liberal | 1916–22 |
| Andrew Bonar Law | Conservative | 1922–23 |
| Stanley Baldwin | Conservative | 1923, 1924–29, 1935–37 |
| Ramsay MacDonald | Labour | 1924, 1929–35 |
| Neville Chamberlain | Conservative | 1937–40 |
| Sir Winston Churchill | Conservative | 1940–45, 1951–55 |
| Clement Attlee | Labour | 1945–51 |
| Sir Anthony Eden | Conservative | 1955–57 |
| Harold Macmillan | Conservative | 1957–63 |
| Sir Alec Douglas-Home | Conservative | 1963–64 |
| Harold Wilson | Labour | 1964–70, 1974–76 |
| Edward Heath | Conservative | 1970–74 |
| James Callaghan | Labour | 1976–79 |
| Margaret Thatcher | Conservative | 1979–90 |
| John Major | Conservative | 1990–97 |
| Tony Blair | Labour | 1997–2007 |
| Gordon Brown | Labour | 2007–10 |
| David Cameron | Conservative | 2010–16 |
| Theresa May | Conservative | 2016–present |

# PRESIDENTS OF THE USA SINCE 1900

| PRESIDENT | PARTY | TERM IN OFFICE |
|---|---|---|
| William McKinley | Republican | 1897–1901 |
| Theodore Roosevelt | Republican | 1901–9 |
| William H. Taft | Republican | 1909–13 |
| Woodrow Wilson | Democrat | 1913–21 |
| Warren G. Harding | Republican | 1921–23 |
| Calvin Coolidge | Republican | 1923–29 |
| Herbert Hoover | Republican | 1929–33 |
| Franklin D. Roosevelt | Democrat | 1933–45 |
| Harry S. Truman | Democrat | 1945–53 |
| Dwight D. Eisenhower | Republican | 1953–61 |
| John F. Kennedy | Democrat | 1961–63 |
| Lyndon B. Johnson | Democrat | 1963–69 |
| Richard M. Nixon | Republican | 1969–74 |
| Gerald R. Ford | Republican | 1974–77 |
| Jimmy Carter | Democrat | 1977–81 |
| Ronald Reagan | Republican | 1981–89 |
| George Bush | Republican | 1989–93 |
| Bill Clinton | Democrat | 1993–2001 |
| George W. Bush | Republican | 2001–9 |
| Barack Obama | Democrat | 2009–2017 |
| Donald Trump | Republican | 2017–present |

# SCIENCE AND MEDICINE

# TOP TEN LARGEST HUMAN ORGANS

| | ORGAN | AVERAGE WEIGHT |
|---|---|---|
| 1 | **Skin** | **10,886 g** |
| 2 | Liver | 1,560 g |
| 3 | Brain | 1,263 g |
| 4 | Lungs | 1,090 g |
| 5 | Heart | 300 g |
| 6 | Kidneys | 290 g |
| 7 | Spleen | 170 g |
| 8 | Pancreas | 98 g |
| 9 | Thyroid | 35 g |
| 10 | Prostate | 20 g |

# TOP TEN LONGEST BONES

| | BONE | AVERAGE LENGTH |
|---|---|---|
| 1 | **Femur** | **50.5 cm** |
| 2 | Tibia | 43.03 cm |
| 3 | Fibula | 40.5 cm |
| 4 | Humerus | 36.46 cm |
| 5 | Ulna | 28.2 cm |
| 6 | Radius | 26.42 cm |
| 7 | Seventh rib | 24 cm |
| 8 | Eighth rib | 23 cm |
| 9 | Innominate bone or hipbone | 18.5 cm |
| 10 | Sternum | 17 cm |

# BIG NAMES IN THE SCIENTIFIC AND MEDICAL FIELDS

| NAME | ACHIEVEMENTS |
| --- | --- |
| Archimedes (287–212 BC) | Greek; discovered areas and theories in mathematics that were being developed two millennia later; founded science of hydrostatics. |
| Aristotle (384–322 BC) | Greek; one of the most influential figures in the history of Western thought and scientific tradition. |
| Barnard, Christian (1922–2001) | South African surgeon; performed the first successful heart transplant in December 1967 at Groote Schuur Hospital, South Africa. |
| Bohr, Niels (1885–1962) | Danish physicist; furthered atomic physics; won a Nobel prize for physics in 1922 and assisted in atom bomb research during World War Two. |
| Boyle, Robert (1627–91) | Irish physicist and chemist; Boyle's law in 1662 states that the pressure and volume of a gas are inversely proportional at constant temperature. |
| Copernicus, Nicolaus (1473–1543) | Polish astronomer; published the unpopular theory that the sun is at the centre of the universe in 1543. |
| Curie, Marie (1867–1934) | Polish/French physicist; worked on magnetism and radioactivity isolating radium and polonium. |
| Darwin, Charles (1809–82) | English naturalist; made many geological and zoological discoveries culminating in his theory of evolution which he published in 1859. |

| NAME | ACHIEVEMENTS |
|------|--------------|
| Davy, Humphrey (1778–1829) | English chemist; discovered the anaesthetic effect of laughing gas; discovered the new metals potassium, sodium, barium, strontium, calcium and magnesium; devised safety lamps for miners and was important in promoting science with industry. |
| Einstein, Albert (1879–1955) | German/Swiss/American mathematical physicist; achieved world fame through his special and general theories of relativity. |
| Fleming, Alexander (1881–1955) | Scottish bacteriologist; first to use antityphoid vaccines on humans; pioneered the use of salvarsan to treat syphilis; in 1928, discovered penicillin by chance. |
| Galileo (1564–1642) | Italian astronomer, mathematician and natural philosopher; deduced the value of a pendulum for exact measurement of time; proved that all falling bodies, great or small, descend due to gravity at the same rate; perfected the refracting telescope; was convinced by the Copernican theory, which led to his imprisonment. |
| Harvey, William (1578–1657) | English physician; discovered the circulation of blood. |
| Newton, Isaac (1642–1727) | English scientist and mathematician; formulated complete theory of gravitation by 1684; also carried out important work in optics. |
| Pasteur, Louis (1822–95) | French chemist, father of modern bacteriology, introduced pasteurization. |
| Pavlov, Petrovich (1849–1936) | Russian physiologist; studied physiology of circulation and digestion; 'conditioned' or acquired reflexes. |
| Röntgen, Wilhelm (1845–1923) | German physicist; discovered electromagnetic rays, which he named X-rays, in 1895. |

| NAME | ACHIEVEMENTS |
|------|--------------|
| Schrödinger, Erwin (1887–1961) | Austrian physicist; originated the study of wave mechanics as part of the quantum theory with the celebrated Schrödinger wave equation. |
| Thomson, Joseph (1856–1940) | English physicist; studied gaseous conductors of electricity and the nature of cathode rays, which led to his discovery of the electron; also discovered the existence of isotopes of elements. |
| Volta, Alessandro (1745–1827) | Italian physicist; developed the theory of current electricity; invented an electric battery and discovered the electric composition of water; the electrical 'volt' is named after him. |
| Watt, James (1736–1819) | Scottish engineer and inventor; developed and improved early models of the steam engine; the watt, a unit of power, is named after him and the term horsepower was first used by him. |

# GREAT MEDICAL DISCOVERIES

| DISCOVERY | SCIENTIST | YEAR |
|-----------|-----------|------|
| Anaesthetic (chloroform) | James Young Simpson | 1847 |
| Anaesthetic (ether) | William Morton | 1846 |
| Antiseptic surgery | Joseph Lister | 1865 |
| Aspirin | Hermann Dreser / Felix Hoffman | 1899 |
| Atrophine | Rudolph Brondes | 1819 |

| DISCOVERY | SCIENTIST | YEAR |
|---|---|---|
| Bacteria | Anton van Leeuwenhoek | 1674 |
| Circulation of blood | William Harvey | 1628 |
| Digitalis | William Withering | 1785 |
| Diphtheria bacillus | Edwin Klebs | 1884 |
| DNA | Francis Crick and James Watson | 1953 |
| Germ theory | John Snow | 1854 |
| HIV virus identified | Luc Montagnier | 1983 |
| Insulin (treatment for diabetes) | Frederick Banting and Charles Best | 1921 |
| IVF | Patrick Steptoe and Robert Edwards | 1978 |
| Morphine | Friedrich Sertürner | 1805 |
| Pacemaker | Paul Zoll | 1952 |
| Pasteurization | Louis Pasteur | 1861 |
| Penicillin | Alexander Fleming | 1928 |
| Rabies vaccine | Louis Pasteur | 1885 |
| Salvarsan (bacterial agent) | Paul Ehrlich | 1910 |
| Tuberculosis bacillus | Robert Koch | 1882 |
| Vaccination (against smallpox) | Edward Jenner | 1796 |
| Viruses | Martinus Beijerinck | 1897 |
| Whooping cough bacillus | Jules Bordet | 1906 |
| X-rays | Wilhelm Röntgen | 1895 |

# THE PH SYSTEM*

| SUBSTANCE | PH LISTING |
| --- | --- |
| Hydrochloric acid | 0 |
| Car battery acid | 1 |
| Digestive juices | 1–3 |
| Lime juice | 2.3 |
| Vinegar | 3 |
| Orange juice | 3.7 |
| Normal rainfall | 5.6 |
| Saliva | 6.4–6.9 |
| Milk | 6.6 |
| Pure water | 7 |
| Human blood | 7.4 |
| Sea water | 7.8–8.3 |

* The pH system was invented in 1909 by Danish chemist Søren Sørensen, and involves the measurement of the concentration of hydrogen ions. In turn, this tells us how acidic or alkaline a substance is – pH testing is traditionally performed using litmus paper

# HIGHEST MELTING POINTS

| | SUBSTANCE | TEMP IN °C | TEMP IN °F |
| --- | --- | --- | --- |
| 1 | **Carbon** | **3,527°C** | **6,381°F** |
| 2 | Tungsten | 3,422°C | 6,192°F |
| 3 | Rhenium | 3,186°C | 5,767°F |
| 4 | Osmium | 3,033°C | 5,491°F |
| 5 | Tantalum | 3,017°C | 5,463°F |

# DECIPHERING DOCTORS' NOTES...

| DIAGNOSIS | DESCRIPTION |
|---|---|
| Anaemia | Lack of red blood corpuscles |
| Anosma | Loss of sense of smell |
| Appendicitis | Inflammation of the appendix |
| Arthritis | Inflammation of a joint |
| Astigmatism | Eye defect affecting focusing |
| Aural | Of the ear |
| Brachial | Of the arm |
| Bronchitis | Inflammation of the lining of the bronchial tubes |
| Buccal | Of the cheek, mouth |
| Bursitis | Inflammation of a bursa (tennis elbow) |
| Cardiac | Of the heart |
| Cerebral | Of the brain |
| Cholecystitis | Inflammation of the gall bladder |
| Claudication | Lameness |
| Colitis | Inflammation of the colon |
| Conjunctivitis | Inflammation of the conjunctiva |
| Cranial | Of the skull |
| Cystitis | Inflammation of the bladder |
| Daltonism | Colour blindness |
| Dermatitis | Inflammation of the skin |
| Digital | Of the fingers |
| Diplopia | Double vision |
| Dyspepsia | Indigestion |
| Encephalitis | Inflammation of the brain |
| Epistaxis | Nose bleed |
| Erythrocytes | Red blood corpuscles |
| Fibrositis | Inflammation of the fibrous tissue |
| Genal | Of the cheeks |

| DIAGNOSIS | DESCRIPTION |
|---|---|
| Genial | Of the chin |
| Gingivitis | Inflammation of the gums |
| Glossitis | Inflammation of the tongue |
| Haematic | Of the blood |
| Hemicrania | Migraine |
| Hepatic | Of the liver |
| Hepatitis | Inflammation of the liver |
| Herpes zoster | Shingles |
| Hypermetropia | Long-sightedness |
| Infectious mononucleosis | Glandular fever |
| Keratitis | Inflammation of the cornea |
| Laryngitis | Inflammation of the larynx |
| Leucocytes | White blood corpuscles |
| Mastitis | Inflammation of the mammary gland |
| Meningitis | Inflammation of the membranes surrounding the brain |
| Metopic | Of the forehead |
| Myopia | Short-sightedness |
| Nasal | Of the nose |
| Nephritis | Inflammation of the kidney |
| Neuritis | Inflammation of the nerves |
| Occipital | Of the back of the head |
| Opthalmic | Of the eye |
| Oral | Of the mouth |
| Osteitis | Inflammation of a bone |
| Otitis | Inflammation of the ear |
| Parotitis | Mumps |
| Pectoral | Of the chest |
| Pedal | Of the foot |
| Peritonitis | Inflammation of the peritoneum |
| Pertussis | Whooping cough |

| DIAGNOSIS | DESCRIPTION |
| --- | --- |
| Phagocytes | White blood cells that fight disease by engulfing bacteria |
| Pharyngitis | Inflammation of the mucous membrane of the pharynx |
| Phlebitis | Inflammation of a vein |
| Pollenosis | Hay fever |
| Pulmonary | Of the lungs |
| Renal | Of the kidneys |
| Rhinitis | Inflammation of the mucous membrane of the nose |
| Rubella | German measels |
| Scarlatina | Scarlet fever |
| Spondylitis | Inflammation of a vertebra |
| Sternutation | Sneezing |
| Stomatitis | Inflammation of the mucous membrane of the mouth |
| Strabismus | Squint |
| Syncope | Fainting |
| Tarsal | Of the ankle |
| Tonsillitis | Inflammation of the tonsils |
| Traulism | A stammer |
| Varicella | Chicken pox |
| Volar | Of the palm of the hand, sole of the foot |

# THE HUMAN BODY IN NUMBERS

**206** bones in an adult human

**33** vertebrae

**27** bones in the hand

**26** bones in the foot

**24** ribs (12 sets)

# I'VE BROKEN MY...

| MEDICAL NAME | COMMON NAME |
| --- | --- |
| Cranium | Skull |
| Malar/zygomatic bone | Cheek |
| Maxilla | Upper jaw |
| Mandible | Lower jaw |
| Clavicle | Collar bone |
| Scapula | Shoulder blade |
| Sternum | Breast bone |
| Humerus | Upper arm |
| Radius | Lower arm |
| Ulna | Lower arm |
| Carpus | Wrist |
| Metacarpus | Hand |
| Pollex | Thumb |
| Phalanges | Fingers, toes |
| Ilium | Hip |
| Femur | Thigh bone (longest bone in body) |
| Patella | Knee cap |
| Tibia | Shin bone |
| Fibula | Calf bone |
| Talus | Ankle |
| Metatarsus | Foot |

# SCIENTIFIC DISCOVERIES OF THE TWENTIETH AND TWENTY-FIRST CENTURIES

- In 1917, Ernest Rutherford was the first man to split the atom.
- In 1934, Enrico Fermi and collaborators discovered that bombarding uranium with neutrons leads to the production of new radioactive material and a potential new source of energy.
- In 2001, the first draft of the human genome was completed.
- In 2007, scientists learned how to reprogramme skin cells into stem cells, without cloning or destroying embryos.
- In May 2010, J. Craig Venter Institute created the world's first self-replicating, synthetic bacterial cell proving, in principle, that genomes can be designed by computer and chemically made in a laboratory. This could lead to the design of bacterial cells that produce medicines and fuels and even absorb greenhouse gases.

# CHEMICAL ELEMENTS

| CHEMICAL SYMBOL | SUBSTANCE | CHEMICAL SYMBOL | SUBSTANCE |
| --- | --- | --- | --- |
| Ag | Silver | Mn | Manganese |
| Al | Aluminium | N | Nitrogen |
| Ar | Argon | Na | Sodium |
| As | Arsenic | Ne | Neon |
| Au | Gold | Ni | Nickel |
| B | Boron | O | Oxygen |
| Ba | Barium | Os | Osmium |
| Br | Bromine | P | Phosphorus |

| CHEMICAL SYMBOL | SUBSTANCE | CHEMICAL SYMBOL | SUBSTANCE |
|---|---|---|---|
| C | Carbon | Pb | Lead |
| Ca | Calcium | Pt | Platinum |
| Cl | Chlorine | Pu | Plutonium |
| Co | Cobalt | Ra | Radium |
| Cr | Chromium | Rn | Radon |
| Cu | Copper | S | Sulphur |
| F | Fluorine | Sb | Antimony |
| Fe | Iron | Si | Silicon |
| H | Hydrogen | Sn | Tin |
| He | Helium | Sr | Strontium |
| Hg | Mercury | U | Uranium |
| I | Iodine | W | Tungsten |
| K | Potassium | Xe | Xenon |
| Kr | Krypton | Zn | Zinc |
| Li | Lithium | Zr | Zirconium |
| Mg | Magnesium | | |

## Fascinating Facts

- Osmium is the heaviest element, weighing in at 22.61 g/cm³. It was discovered in 1803 and one of its uses is for the nibs of fountain pens.

- One kilogram of plutonium would produce an explosion equivalent to 20,000 tons of TNT.

- The half-life of uranium-238 (the most common isotope) is 4.46 billion years, roughly on par with the age of the earth.

# SPACE AND ASTRONOMY

# TOP TEN FAMOUS COMETS THROUGHOUT HISTORY

1   **Halley's Comet – first observed in 1682 – orbits earth every 75 to 76 years.**

2   Shoemaker Levy-9 – destroyed in 1994 – size unknown (one fragment was 1.2 miles long). Erratic orbit of Jupiter lasted two years.

3   Hyakutake – sighted in March 1996 – approx. 350 million miles long (570 million km). Orbit lasts approx. 100,000 years.

4   Hale Bopp – first observed in 1995 – nucleus has a diameter of 24 miles (40 km). Orbit lasts approx. 2,500 years.

5   Comet Borrelly – first observed in 1904 – nucleus is 5 miles (8 km) long.

6   Comet Encke – first observed in 1819 – nucleus has a diameter of 3 miles (4.8 km). Orbit lasts three years.

7   Tempel-Tuttel – first observed in 1865 – approx. 3.1 miles (5 km) in diameter.

8   Comet Tempel 1 – first observed in 1867 – approx. 3.7 miles (6 km) long. Orbit lasts six years.

9   Comet Wild 2 – first observed in 1978 – approx. 3.1 miles (5 km) in diameter. An orbit lasts six years.

10  Churyumov-Gerasimenko – first observed in 1969 – approx. 3.1 miles (5 km) across and currently orbits the sun about every six years.

## Fascinating Facts

- Shoemaker Levy-9 was destroyed when it collided with Jupiter, breaking into 21 pieces. Just one of these fragments generated an explosion equivalent to 6 million megatonnes of TNT.
- Comet Borrelly is shaped like a giant bowling pin.

# MEN ON THE MOON (BY MISSION)

| SHUTTLE MISSION | DATE | ASTRONAUTS |
|---|---|---|
| Apollo 11 | 20 July 1969 | Neil Armstrong, Buzz Aldrin |
| Apollo 12 | 19 November 1969 | Charles Conrad, Alan Bean |
| Apollo 14 | 5 February 1971 | Alan Shepard, Edgar Mitchell |
| Apollo 15 | 30 July 1971 | James Irwin, David Scott |
| Apollo 16 | 21 April 1972 | Charles Duke, John Young |
| Apollo 17 | 11 December 1972 | Harrison Schmitt, Eugene Cernan |

## Fascinating Facts

- A 'blue moon' is the second of two full moons that fall in the same month. Full moons take place roughly every 29.5 days, so a blue moon occurs approximately every 2.75 years.

- The largest crater on our moon measures 2,100 km in diameter and is 12 km deep.

 # SPACE EXPLORATION FIRSTS

**First woman in space** – Valentina Tereshkova in Vostok 6 for USSR on 16 June 1963

**First Brit in space** – Helen Sharman in Soyuz TM-12 for RKA agency on 18 May 1991

**First monkey in space** – Albert II (died on re-impact with earth) in V2 for NASA on 14 June 1949

**First person to complete a marathon in space** – American astronaut Sunita Williams ran the Boston marathon on a treadmill aboard the International Space Station on 16 April 2007

 # PLANETS IN ORDER OF PROXIMITY TO THE SUN

| PLANET | PROXIMITY TO THE SUN |
| --- | --- |
| Mercury | 36 million miles |
| Venus | 67 million miles |
| Earth | 93 million miles |
| Mars | 142 million miles |
| Jupiter | 483 million miles |
| Saturn | 886 million miles |
| Uranus | 1,783 million miles |
| Neptune | 2,793 million miles |

## Fascinating Facts

- Pluto was stripped of its planetary status in August 2006. To qualify as a planet, it must orbit around the sun, be round in shape and have an orbit of its own clear of other planets. Pluto was disqualified because its orbit overlaps with that of Neptune.

- All the planets are named after Greco-Roman gods – for example, the largest planet, Jupiter, is named after the king of the gods, and the 'blue planet' Neptune, after the god of the sea.

- Astronomers have found the most earth-like planet outside our Solar System to date, a world which could have water running on its surface. The planet orbits the faint star Gliese 581, which is 20.5 light years away in the constellation Libra. Scientists say that the benign temperatures on the planet mean any water there could exist in liquid form, and this raises the chances it could also harbour life.

 **THE SUN IN NUMBERS**

**½ a billionth** – the amount of the sun's energy which actually reaches earth.

**8** – the time in minutes it takes for light from the sun to reach earth. If the sun fizzled out, the planet would still be illuminated for 8 minutes afterwards.

**1,950** – how many times bigger the diameter of the star VY Canis Majoris is than that of the sun.

**149,597,893** – how many kilometres the sun is from earth.

**15 million** – how many degrees cent grade the sun measures at its core.

**10 billion** – the length of the sun's lifetime in years. It is currently middle-aged.

**TOP TEN ANNUAL METEOR SHOWERS**

| | NAME | SEEN |
|---|---|---|
| 1 | Quadrantids | 1–6 January |
| 2 | Lyrids | 19–22 April |
| 3 | Eta Aquarids | 1–8 May |
| 4 | Delta Aquarids | 15 July–10 August |
| 5 | Perseids | 27 July–17 August |
| 6 | Orionids | 15–25 October |
| 7 | Leonids | 14–20 November |
| 8 | Andromedids | 26 November–4 December |
| 9 | Geminids | 9–13 December |
| 10 | Ursids | 20–22 December |

# SPORT

# TOP TEN MOST POPULAR SPORTS*

| | SPORT | ESTIMATED NUMBER OF FANS |
|---|---|---|
| **1** | **Soccer** | **3.5 billion** |
| 2 | Cricket | 2.5 billion |
| 3 | Field hockey | 2 billion |
| 4 | Tennis | 1 billion |
| 5 | Volleyball | 900 million |
| 6 | Table tennis | 850 million |
| 7 | Baseball | 500 million |
| 8 | Golf | 450 million |
| 9 | Basketball | 400 million |
| 10 | American football | 400 million |

* As calculated by Internet use

## Fascinating Fact

- Boxing became a legal sport in 1901.

# TOP 10 CRICKETERS WITH MOST WICKETS TAKEN IN THEIR TEST-MATCH CAREER*

|    | NAME | COUNTRY | WICKETS |
|----|------|---------|---------|
| 1  | **Muttiah Muralitharan** | **Sri Lanka** | **800** |
| 2  | Shane Warne | Australia | 708 |
| 3  | Anil Kumble | India | 619 |
| 4  | Glenn McGrath | Australia | 563 |
| 5  | Courtney Walsh | West Indies | 519 |
| 6  | James Anderson | England | 467 |
| 7  | Kapil Dev | India | 434 |
| 8  | Richard Hadlee | New Zealand | 431 |
| 9  | Shaun Pollock | South Africa | 421 |
| 10 | Dale Steyn | South Africa | 417 |

* As of November 2016

# CRICKET WORLD CUP WINNERS

| YEAR | COUNTRY |
| --- | --- |
| 1975 | West Indies |
| 1979 | West Indies |
| 1983 | India |
| 1987 | Australia |
| 1992 | Pakistan |
| 1996 | Sri Lanka |
| 1999 | Australia |
| 2003 | Australia |
| 2007 | Australia |
| 2011 | India |
| 2015 | Australia |

## Fascinating Facts

- Australia's Glenn McGrath has taken the most number of wickets in World Cup cricket history with 71.

- The first international cricket match ever held was between Canada and the USA in September 1844.

# TOP TEN CRICKETERS WITH THE MOST CENTURIES IN TEST MATCH CRICKET*

| 1 | Sachin Tendulkar, India: 51 from 200 matches |
|---|---|
| 2 | Jacques Kallis, South Africa: 45 from 166 matches |
| 3 | Ricky Ponting, Australia: 41 from 168 matches |
| 4 | Kumar Sangakkara, Sri Lanka: 38 from 134 matches |
| 5 | Rahul Dravid, India: 36 from 164 matches |
| 6 | Sunil Gavaskar, India: 34 from 125 matches |
| 7 | Brian Lara, West Indies: 34 from 131 matches |
| 8 | Mahela Jayawardene, Sri Lanka: 34 from 149 matches |
| 9 | Steve Waugh, Australia: 32 from 168 matches |
| 10 | Younis Khan, Pakistan: 31 from 104 matches |

* As of June 2016

# THE FIFA WORLD CUP IN NUMBERS

**3** – The number of winners' medals won by Pelé for Brazil in the years 1958, 1962 and 1970.

**3** – The most goals scored in a final by a single player – Geoff Hurst for England vs West Germany in 1966.

**5** – The most goals scored by one player in a single match – Oleg Salenko for Russia vs Cameroon in 1994.

**8** – The number of tournaments in which Scotland hasn't advanced from the first round.

**11** – The duration in seconds of the fastest goal – scored by Hakan Şükür for Turkey vs South Korea in 2002.

**43** – The age of the oldest World Cup player – Columbian goalkeeper Faryd Mondragón in a 4–1 win over Japan in 2014.

# TOP TEN FOOTBALLING NATIONS (FIFA RANKING)*

| | COUNTRY | FIFA POINTS |
|---|---|---|
| **1** | **Argentina** | **1,585** |
| 2 | Belgium | 1,401 |
| 3 | Colombia | 1,331 |
| 4 | Germany | 1,319 |
| 5 | Chile | 1316 |
| 6 | Portugal | 1,266 |
| 7 | France | 1,189 |
| 8 | Spain | 1,165 |
| 9 | Brazil | 1,156 |
| 10 | Italy | 1,155 |

\* Ranked in FIFA points total, as of July 2016

# TOP TEN MOST CAPPED FIFA WORLD CUP FINALISTS*

| | NAME | COUNTRY | NO. OF CAPS IN WORLD CUP |
|---|---|---|---|
| 1 | **Lothar Matthäus** | **Germany / West Germany** | **25** |
| 2 | Miroslav Klose | Germany | 24 |
| 3 | Paolo Maldini | Italy | 23 |
| =4 | Diego Maradona | Argentina | 21 |
| =4 | Władysław Żmuda | Poland | 21 |
| =4 | Uwe Seeler | Germany / West Germany | 21 |
| =7 | Grzegorz Lato | Poland | 20 |
| =7 | Cafu | Brazil | 20 |
| =7 | Philipp Lahm | Germany | 20 |
| =7 | Bastian Schweinsteiger | Germany | 20 |

* Listed by number of appearances

# TOP TEN MOST CAPPED ENGLAND FOOTBALL PLAYERS*

| | NAME | NO. OF CAPS |
|---|---|---|
| **1** | **Peter Shilton** | **125** |
| =2 | David Beckham | 115 |
| =2 | Wayne Rooney | 115 |
| 4 | Steven Gerrard | 114 |
| 5 | Bobby Moore | 108 |
| 6 | Ashley Cole | 107 |
| =7 | Bobby Charlton | 106 |
| =7 | Frank Lampard | 106 |
| 9 | Billy Wright | 105 |
| 10 | Bryan Robson | 90 |

\* As of July 2016

# MOST CONSECUTIVE MINUTES WITHOUT CONCEDING A WORLD CUP GOAL

559 – Switzerland – 2 July 1994 to 21 June 2010

549 – Italy – 17 June 1986 to 3 July 1990

500 – England – 16 June 1982 to 3 June 1986

# TOP TEN MOST EXPENSIVE FOOTBALL PLAYERS IN TRANSFER FEES*

| | NAME | TRANSFER | FEE |
|---|---|---|---|
| 1 | **Paul Pogba** | **Juventus to Manchester United** | **£89.3 million (2016)** |
| 2 | Gareth Bale | Tottenham Hotspur to Real Madrid | £85.1 million (2013) |
| 3 | Cristiano Ronaldo | Manchester United to Real Madrid | £80 million (2009) |
| 4 | Gonzalo Higuaín | Napoli to Juventus | £75.3 million (2016) |
| 5 | Luis Suárez | Liverpool to Barcelona | £65 million (2014) |
| 6 | James Rodríguez | AS Monaco to Real Madrid | £63 million (2014) |
| 7 | Ángel Di María | Real Madrid to Manchester United | £59.7 million (2014) |
| 8 | Zlatan Ibrahimović | Inter to Barcelona | £59 million (2009) |
| 9 | Kevin De Bruyne | Wolfsburg to Manchester City | £55 million (2015) |
| 10 | Kaká | AC Milan to Real Madrid | £56 million (2009) |

* As of October 2016

# TOP TEN ENGLAND GOALSCORERS (FOOTBALL)

| | NAME | NO. OF GOALS |
|---|---|---|
| 1 | **Wayne Rooney (2003–present)** | **53 (115 caps)** |
| 2 | Bobby Charlton (1958–1970) | 49 (106 caps) |
| 3 | Gary Lineker (1984–1992) | 48 (80 caps) |
| 4 | Jimmy Greaves (1959–1967) | 44 (57 caps) |
| 5 | Michael Owen (1998–2008) | 40 (89 caps) |
| =6 | Tom Finney (1946–1958) | 30 (76 caps) |
| =6 | Alan Shearer (1992–2000) | 30 (63 caps) |
| =6 | Nat Lofthouse (1950–1958) | 30 (33 caps) |
| =9 | Frank Lampard (2003–2013) | 29 (106 caps) |
| =9 | Vivian Woodward (1903–1911) | 29 (23 caps) |

# TOP TEN WEALTHIEST CLUBS*

| 1 | **Real Madrid, Spain – £2.17 billion** |
|---|---|
| 2 | FC Barcelona, Spain – £2.1 billion |
| 3 | Manchester United, England – £2.03 billion |
| 4 | Bayern Munich, Germany – £1.51 billion |
| 5 | Manchester City, England – £910 million |
| 6 | Chelsea, England – £900 million |
| 7 | Arsenal, England – £850 million |
| 8 | Liverpool, England – £646 million |
| 9 | Juventas, Italy – £550 million |
| 10 | AC Milan, Italy – £510 million |

* As of July 2016

# TOP TEN MOST SUCCESSFUL ENGLAND FOOTBALL MANAGERS*

| | NAME | SUCCESS RATE |
|---|---|---|
| 1 | **Sam Allardyce (2016)** | **Won 100 per cent of 1 match** |
| 2 | Fabio Capello (2008–2011) | Won 66.7 per cent of 42 matches |
| 3 | Alf Ramsey (1963–1974) | Won 61.1 per cent of 113 matches |
| 4 | Glenn Hoddle (1996–1999) | Won 61 per cent of 28 matches |
| 5 | Ron Greenwood (1977–1982) | Won 60 per cent of 55 matches |
| 6 | Sven-Göran Eriksson (2001–2006) | Won 59.7 per cent of 67 matches |
| 7 | Roy Hodgson (2012–2016) | Won 58.9 percent of 56 matches |
| 8 | Walter Winterbottom (1946–1962) | Won 56.1 per cent of 139 matches |
| 9 | Steve McLaren (2006–2007) | Won 50 per cent of 18 matches |
| 10 | Bobby Robson (1982–1990) | Won 49.5 per cent of 95 matches |

* As of October 2016

# TOP TEN WEALTHIEST PLAYERS*

| 1 | **Cristiano Ronaldo – Portugal, Real Madrid – $230 million** |
|---|---|
| 2 | Lionel Messi – Argentina, Barcelona – $218 million |
| 3 | Neymar – Brazil, Barcelona – $148 million |
| 4 | Zlatan Ibrahimović – Sweden, Manchester United – $114 million |
| 5 | Wayne Rooney – England, Manchester United – $112 million |
| 6 | Kaká – Brazil, Orlando City – $108 million |
| =7 | Samuel Eto'o – Cameroon, Anzhi Makhachkala – $95 million |
| =7 | Raul, Spain, New York Cosmos – $95 million |
| 9 | Ronaldinho – Brazil, Querétaro FC – $93 million |
| 10 | Frank Lampard – England, New York City FC – $85 million |

\* Estimated net worth in 2016

# TOP TEN HIGHEST PAID
# FOOTBALL MANAGERS*

| 1 | **Pep Guardiola (Manchester City) – £15 million** |
|---|---|
| 2 | José Mourinho (Manchester United) – £13.8 million |
| 3 | Carlo Ancelotti (Bayern Munich) – £9 million |
| 4 | Arsene Wenger (Arsenal) – £8.3 million |
| 5 | Zinedine Zidane (Real Madrid) – £8 million |
| =6 | Jurgen Klopp (Liverpool) – £7 million |
| =6 | Luis Enrique (FC Barcelona) – £7 million |
| 8 | Antonio Conte (Chelsea) – £6.5 million |
| 9 | Maurico Pochettino (Tottenham) – £5.5 million |
| 10 | Rafael Benitez (Newcastle United) – £4.5 million |

\* Refers to salary in 2016

# TOP TEN OLDEST FOOTBALL CLUBS IN UK LEAGUE

| | TEAM | YEAR FOUNDED |
|---|---|---|
| 1 | **Notts County** | **1862** |
| 2 | Stoke City | 1863 |
| 3 | Nottingham Forest | 1865 |
| 4 | Chesterfield | 1866 |
| 5 | Sheffield Wednesday | 1867 |
| 6 | Reading | 1871 |
| 7 | Wrexham | 1873 |
| =8 | Aston Villa | 1874 |
| =8 | Bolton Wanderers | 1874 |
| 10 | Birmingham City | 1875 |

 FIFA WORLD CUP GOLDEN BOOT WINNERS

| YEAR | NAME | TEAM | NO. OF GOALS SCORED |
|---|---|---|---|
| 1970 | Gerd Müller | West Germany | 10 |
| 1974 | Grzegorz Lato | Poland | 7 |
| 1978 | Mario Kempes | Argentina | 6 |
| 1982 | Paolo Rossi | Italy | 6 |
| 1986 | Gary Lineker | England | 6 |
| 1990 | Salvatore Schillaci | Italy | 6 |
| 1994 | Oleg Salenko | Russia | 6 |
| 1998 | Davor Šuker | Croatia | 6 |
| 2002 | Ronaldo | Brazil | 8 |
| 2006 | Miroslav Klose | Germany | 5 |
| 2010 | Thomas Müller | Germany | 5 |
| 2014 | James Rodríguez | Columbia | 6 |

# FIFA WORLD PLAYER OF THE YEAR WINNERS*

| YEAR | NAME | NATIONALITY |
| --- | --- | --- |
| 2006 | Fabio Cannavaro | Italy |
| 2007 | Kaká | Brazil |
| 2008 | Ronaldo | Portugal |
| 2009 | Lionel Messi | Argentina |
| 2010 | Lionel Messi | Argentina |
| 2011 | Lionel Messi | Argentina |
| 2012 | Lionel Messi | Argentina |
| 2013 | Cristiano Ronaldo | Portugal |
| 2014 | Cristiano Ronaldo | Portugal |
| 2015 | Lionel Messi | Argentina |

* Since 2010, the world's best male player has been awarded the FIFA Ballon d'Or

 # FIFA WORLD CUP WINNING NATIONS

| COUNTRY | NUMBER OF WINS |
| --- | --- |
| **Brazil** | **5** |
| Italy | 4 |
| Germany | 4 |
| Uruguay | 2 |
| Argentina | 2 |
| England | 1 |
| France | 1 |
| Spain | 1 |

# TOP TEN LARGEST FOOTBALL STADIUMS BY CAPACITY

| | NAME | CAPACITY |
|---|---|---|
| **1** | **Rungrado May Day Stadium, Pyongyang, North Korea** | **150,000** |
| 2 | Estadio Azteca, Mexico City, Mexico | 105,000 |
| 3 | Bukit Jalil National Stadium, Kuala Lumpur, Malaysia | 100,200 |
| 4 | Melbourne Cricket Ground (MG or The G), Melbourne, Australia | 100,000 |
| 5 | Camp Nou, Barcelona, Spain | 99,354 |
| 6 | FNB Stadium (Soccer City), Johannesburg, South Africa | 95,000 |
| 7 | Azadi Stadium, Tehran, Iran | 91,000 |
| 8 | Wembley Stadium, London, UK | 90,000 |
| 9 | Estádio Mário Filho, Rio de Janeiro, Brazil | 88,992 |
| 10 | Gelora Bung Karno Stadium, Central Jakarta, Indonesia | 88,306 |

# TOP TEN FOOTBALL PLAYERS WITH MOST GOALS SCORED IN PREMIER LEAGUE*

| | NAME | NO. OF GOALS |
|---|---|---|
| 1 | **Alan Shearer** | **260** |
| 2 | Wayne Rooney | 188 |
| 3 | Andrew Cole | 187 |
| 4 | Frank Lampard | 177 |
| 5 | Thierry Henry | 175 |
| 6 | Robbie Fowler | 163 |
| 7 | Michael Owen | 150 |
| 8 | Les Ferdinand | 149 |
| 9 | Teddy Sheringham | 146 |
| 10 | Robin van Persie | 144 |

\* Up to end of season 2015/16

# TOP TEN MOST APPEARANCES IN THE PREMIER LEAGUE*

| 1 | **Ryan Giggs** | **632** |
|---|---|---|
| 2 | Frank Lampard | 609 |
| 3 | Gareth Barry | 595 |
| 4 | David James | 572 |
| 5 | Gary Speed | 534 |
| 6 | Emile Heskey | 516 |
| 7 | Mark Schwarzer | 514 |
| 8 | Jamie Carragher | 508 |
| 9 | Phil Neville | 505 |
| 10 | Steven Gerrard | 504 |

\* As of June 2016

# PREMIER LEAGUE FOOTBALL PLAYERS WITH THE MOST RED CARDS*

| | |
|---|---|
| **Richard Dunne** | **8** |
| **Duncan Ferguson** | **8** |
| **Patrick Vieira** | **8** |
| Roy Keane | 7 |
| Lee Cattermole | 7 |
| Alan Smith | 6 |
| Nicky Butt | 6 |
| Eric Cantona | 6 |
| Andrew Cole | 6 |
| Steven Gerrard | 6 |

* As of June 2016 – ten other players not shown on the list have also received six red cards

# TOP TEN PREMIER LEAGUE CLUB PERFORMERS*

| | TEAM | PREMIER LEAGUE POINTS |
|---|---|---|
| **1** | **Manchester United** | **1,952** |
| 2 | Arsenal | 1,747 |
| 3 | Chelsea | 1,696 |
| 4 | Liverpool | 1,601 |
| 5 | Tottenham | 1,361 |
| 6 | Everton | 1,263 |
| 7 | Aston Villa | 1,223 |
| 8 | Newcastle | 1,183 |
| 9 | Manchester City | 1,093 |
| 10 | Blackburn | 970 |

* As of June 2016

# TOP TEN F1 DRIVERS WITH THE MOST WORLD CHAMPIONSHIP TITLES*

| | NAME | COUNTRY | WINS |
|---|---|---|---|
| 1 | **Michael Schumacher** | **Germany** | **7** |
| 2 | Juan Manuel Fangio | Argentina | 5 |
| =3 | Alain Prost | France | 4 |
| =3 | Sebastian Vettel | Germany | 4 |
| =5 | Lewis Hamilton | Great Britain | 3 |
| =5 | Jack Brabham | Australia | 3 |
| =5 | Jackie Stewart | Great Britian | 3 |
| =5 | Niki Lauda | Austria | 3 |
| =5 | Nelson Piquet | Brazil | 3 |
| =5 | Ayrton Senna | Brazil | 3 |

\* As of the start of the 2016 season

# F1 IN NUMBERS

**3,100** – The number of times (on average) a Formula 1 car will change gear during the Monaco Grand Prix.

**1906** – The date that Ferenc Szisz from Romania, driving a Renault, won the first F1 Grand Prix held at Le Mans, France.

**369.9** – The top speed in kilometres per hour of a Formula 1 car.

**46** years **1** month and **11** days – The age of the oldest world champion, Argentina's Juan Manuel Fangio in 1957.

**7** – The number of seconds it takes for an F1 car to go from a standstill to 200 km/h and back again.

**2** – The number of kilograms (on average) a Formula 1 driver will lose during a grand prix.

**1.5** – How many litres of fluid a driver can lose during a hot race.

 # F1 ONE WORLD DRIVERS' CHAMPIONS

| YEAR | NAME | COUNTRY | TEAM | ENGINE |
|---|---|---|---|---|
| 2006 | Fernando Alonso | Spain | Renault | Renault |
| 2007 | Kimi Räikkönen | Finland | Ferrari | Ferrari |
| 2008 | Lewis Hamilton | Great Britain | McLaren | Mercedes |
| 2009 | Jenson Button | Great Britain | Brawn | Mercedes |
| 2010 | Sebastian Vettel | Germany | Red Bull | Renault |
| 2011 | Sebastian Vettel | Germany | Red Bull | Renault |
| 2012 | Sebastian Vettel | Germany | Red Bull | Renault |
| 2013 | Sebastian Vettel | Germany | Red Bull | Renault |
| 2014 | Lewis Hamilton | Great Britain | Mercedes | Mercedes |
| 2015 | Lewis Hamilton | Great Britain | Mercedes | Mercedes |

# TOP TEN FASTEST WOMEN'S MARATHON TIMES*

|     | NAME | COUNTRY | MARATHON | TIME |
| --- | --- | --- | --- | --- |
| 1 | **Paula Radcliffe** | **Great Britain** | **London on 13 April 2003** | **2:15:25** |
| 2 | Paula Radcliffe | Great Britain | Chicago on 13 October 2002 | 2:17:18 |
| 3 | Paula Radcliffe | Great Britain | London on 17 April 2005 | 2:17:42 |
| 4 | Mary Keitany | Kenya | London on 22 April 2012 | 2:18:37 |
| 5 | Catherine Ndereba | Kenya | Chicago on 7 October 2001 | 2:18:47 |
| 6 | Paula Radcliffe | Great Britain | London on 14 April 2002 | 2:18:56 |
| 7 | Rita Sitienei Jeptoo | Kenya | Boston on 21 April 2014 | 2:18:57 |
| 8 | Tiki Gelana | Ethiopia | Rotterdam on 15 April 2012 | 2:18:58 |
| 9 | Mizuki Noguchi | Japan | Berlin on 25 Septeber 2005 | 2:19:12 |
| 10 | Irina Mikitenko | Germany | Berlin on 28 September 2008 | 2:19:19 |

* As of June 2016

# TOP TEN FASTEST MEN'S MARATHON TIMES*

| | NAME | COUNTRY | MARATHON | TIME |
|---|---|---|---|---|
| 1 | **Dennis Kimetto** | **Kenya** | **Berlin on 28 September 2014** | **2:02:57** |
| 2 | Geoffrey Mutai | Kenya | Boston on 18 April 2011 | 2:03:02 |
| 3 | Eliud Kipchoge | Kenya | London on 24 April 2016 | 2:03:05 |
| 4 | Moses Mosop | Kenya | Boston on 18 April 2011 | 2:03:06 |
| 5 | Emmanuel Mutai | Kenya | Berlin on 28 September 2014 | 2:03:13 |
| 6 | Wilson Kipsang Kiprotich | Kenya | Berlin on 29 September 2011 | 2:03:23 |
| 7 | Patrick Makau | Kenya | Berlin on 25 September 2011 | 2:03:38 |
| 8 | Wilson Kipsang Kiprotich | Kenya | Frankfurt on 30 October 2011 | 2:03:42 |
| 9 | Dennis Kimetto | Kenya | Chicago on 13 October 2013 | 2:03:45 |
| 10 | Stanley Biwott | Kenya | London on 24 April 2016 | 2:03:51 |

* As of June 2016

# TOP TEN MOST SUCCESSFUL GOLF PLAYERS*

| | NAME | COUNTRY | PERIOD | WINS |
|---|---|---|---|---|
| 1 | **Jack Nicklaus** | **USA** | **1962–1986** | **18** |
| 2 | Tiger Woods | USA | 1997–2008 | 14 |
| 3 | Walter Hagen | USA | 1914–1929 | 11 |
| =4 | Ben Hogan | USA | 1946–1953 | 9 |
| =4 | Gary Player | South Africa | 1959–1978 | 9 |
| 6 | Tom Watson | USA | 1975–1983 | 8 |
| =7 | Gene Sarazen | USA | 1922–1935 | 7 |
| =7 | Bobby Jones | USA | 1923–1930 | 7 |
| =7 | Sam Snead | USA | 1942–1954 | 7 |
| =7 | Arnold Palmer | USA | 1958–1964 | 7 |

\* Based on combined wins of the Masters, the US Open, the Open and the PGA. Harry Vardon, from Jersey, also won seven major tournaments between 1896 and 1914

## Fascinating Facts

- Golf is the only sport to have been played on the moon. On 6 February 1971, astronaut Alan Shepard hit a golf ball on the lunar suface.

- The world's oldest golf course, St Andrews in Scotland, was in use as early as the sixteenth century.

# TOP TEN MEN'S PGA RANKED GOLFERS*

| | NAME | COUNTRY |
|---|---|---|
| 1 | **Jason Day** | **Australia** |
| 3 | Rory McIlroy | Northern Ireland |
| 2 | Dustin Johnson | USA |
| 4 | Henrik Stenson | Sweden |
| 5 | Jordan Spieth | USA |
| 6 | Hideki Matsuyama | Japan |
| 7 | Adam Scott | Australia |
| 8 | Patrick Reed | USA |
| 9 | Alexander Noren | Sweden |
| 10 | Bubba Watson | USA |

* As of 20 November 2016

 # TOP TEN LONGEST UK GOLF COURSES

| | PLACE | LOCATION | YARDS |
|---|---|---|---|
| 1 | **Rockliffe Hall** | **Darlington, England** | **7,897** |
| 2 | The Players Club | Bristol, England | 7,663 |
| 3 | Duke's Course | St Andrews, Scotland | 7,512 |
| 4 | Dalmahoy, East course | Kirknewton, Scotland | 7,475 |
| 5 | The Vale Wales National Course | Hensol, Wales | 7,433 |
| 6 | Turnberry Ailsa | Ayrshire, Scotland | 7,201 |
| 7 | Royal County Down | Newcastle, Northern Ireland | 7,181 |
| 8 | Loch Lomond | Dunbartonshire, Scotland | 7,140 |
| 9 | Woodhall Spa Hotchkin | Lincolnshire, England | 7,080 |
| 10 | Muirfield | East Lothian, Scotland | 7,034 |

# TOP TEN FASTEST MALE RUNNERS (100 METRES)

| | NAME | COUNTRY | TIME |
|---|---|---|---|
| 1 | **Usain Bolt** | **Jamaica** | **9.58 seconds** |
| =2 | Tyson Gay | USA | 9.69 seconds |
| =2 | Yohan Blake | Jamaica | 9.69 seconds |
| 4 | Asafa Powell | Jamaica | 9.72 seconds |
| 5 | Nesta Carter | Jamaica | 9.78 seconds |
| =6 | Maurice Greene | USA | 9.79 seconds |
| =6 | Justin Gatlin | USA | 9.79 seconds |
| 8 | Steve Mullings | Jamaica | 9.80 seconds |
| =9 | Donovan Bailey | Canada | 9.84 seconds |
| =9 | Bruny Surin | Canada | 9.84 seconds |

# TOP TEN FASTEST FEMALE RUNNERS (100 METRES)

| | NAME | COUNTRY | TIME |
|---|---|---|---|
| 1 | **Florence Griffith Joyner** | **USA** | **10.49 seconds** |
| 2 | Carmelita Jeter | USA | 10.64 seconds |
| 3 | Marion Jones | USA | 10.65 seconds |
| 4 | Shelly-Ann Fraser-Pryce | USA | 10.70 seconds |
| 5 | Christine Arron | France | 10.73 seconds |
| 6 | Merlene Ottey | Jamaica | 10.74 seconds |
| 7 | Kerron Stewart | Jamaica | 10.75 seconds |
| =7 | Evelyn Ashford | USA | 10.76 seconds |
| =7 | Veronica Campbell-Brown | Jamaica | 10.76 seconds |
| =9 | Irina Privalova | Russia | 10.77 seconds |
| =9 | Ivet Lalova-Collio | Bulgaria | 10.77 seconds |

# MOST OLYMPIC MEDALS WON BY AN INDIVIDUAL*

| | NAME | COUNTRY | SPORT | TOTAL MEDALS WON (GOLD) |
|---|---|---|---|---|
| 1 | **Michael Phelps** | **USA** | **Swimming** | **28 (23)** |
| 2 | Larisa Latynina | Soviet Union | Gymnastics | 18 (9) |
| 3 | Nikolai Andrianov | Soviet Union | Gymnastics | 15 (7) |
| 4 | Ole Einar Bjørndalen | Norway | Biathlon | 13 (8) |
| 5 | Boris Shakhlin | Soviet Union | Gymnastics | 13 (7) |
| 6 | Edoardo Mangiarotti | Italy | Fencing | 13 (6) |
| 7 | Takashi Ono | Japan | Gymnastics | 13 (5) |
| 8 | Paavo Nurmi | Finland | Athletics | 12 (9) |
| =9 | Birgit Fischer | Germany | Canoeing | 12 (8) |
| =9 | Bjørn Dæhlie | Norway | Cross-country skiing | 12 (8) |

\* As of October 2016

# TOP TEN MOST OLYMPIC GOLD MEDALS WON BY AN INDIVIDUAL

| | NAME | COUNTRY | SPORT | MEDALS WON |
|---|---|---|---|---|
| 1 | **Michael Phelps** | **USA** | **Swimming** | **23** |
| =2 | Larisa Latynina | Soviet Union | Gymnastics | 9 |
| =2 | Paavo Nurmi | Finland | Athletics | 9 |
| =2 | Mark Spitz | USA | Swimming | 9 |
| =2 | Carl Lewis | USA | Athletics | 9 |
| =6 | Bjørn Dæhlie | Norway | Cross-country skiing | 8 |
| =6 | Birgit Fischer | Germany | Canoeing | 8 |
| =6 | Sawao Kato | Japan | Gymnastics | 8 |
| =6 | Jenny Thompson | USA | Swimming | 8 |
| =6 | Ray Ewry | USA | Athletics | 8 |

# TOP TEN MOST OLYMPIC MEDALS WON BY A COUNTRY*

| | COUNTRY | MEDALS WON |
|---|---|---|
| **1** | **USA** | **2,802** |
| 2 | Soviet Union | 1,204 |
| 3 | Great Britain | 873 |
| 4 | Germany | 824 |
| 5 | France | 822 |
| 6 | Italy | 691 |
| 7 | Sweden | 638 |
| 8 | China | 596 |
| 9 | Russia | 567 |
| 10 | East Germany | 519 |

\* Figure indicates total number of summer and winter tournament medals

## Fascinating Facts

- The first modern Olympic Games was held in Athens, Greece, in 1896. There were 311 male, but no female, competitors.

- Badminton's Olympic debut was in 1992 in Barcelona. Since 1992, Asian players have won 42 of the 46 Olympic medals. Over 1.1 billion people watched the first Olympic badminton tournament on television.

- The very first Olympic race, held in 776 BC, was won by Corubus, a chef.

- The first Winter Olympics was held in Chamonix, France, in 1924.

- The Olympic flag was first unveiled at Antwerp in 1920, and was finally retired after the 1984 Games at Los Angeles. A new flag was flown at the 1988 Seoul Games. The five rings in the Olympic flag symbolise the five inhabited continents: Europe, Asia, Africa, Australasia and America. It is believed the colours were chosen because at least one of them can be found in the flag of every nation.

# COUNTRIES WITH THE MOST OLYMPIC GOLDS IN DECATHLON AND HEPTHALON*

| 1 | USA | 14 |
|---|-----|----|
| 2 | Great Britain | 3 |

* As of 2016

# COUNTRIES WITH THE MOST OLYMPIC GOLDS IN BIATHLON*

| 1 | **Russia/Soviet Union** | 19 |
|---|-------------------------|----|
| 2 | Germany | 16 |
| 3 | Norway | 15 |

* Events in a biathlon are cross-country skiing and .22 calibre rifle shooting

# TOP TEN MOST CAPPED RUGBY PLAYERS*

| | NAME | COUNTRY | CAREER | CAPS |
|---|---|---|---|---|
| **1** | **Richie McCaw** | **New Zealand** | **2001–2015** | **148** |
| 2 | Brian O'Driscoll | Ireland, British and Irish Lions | 1999–2014 | 141 |
| 3 | George Gregan | Australia | 1994–2007 | 139 |
| 4 | Keven Mealamu | New Zealand | 2002–2015 | 132 |
| 5 | Gethin Jenkins | Wales, British and Irish Lions | 2002–present | 131 |
| 6 | Ronan O'Gara | Ireland, British and Irish Lions | 2000–2013 | 130 |
| 7 | Victor Matfield | South Africa | 2001–2015 | 127 |
| =8 | Martin Castrogiovanni | Italy | 2002–present | 119 |
| =8 | Jason Leonard | England, British and Irish Lions | 1990–2004 | 119 |
| =8 | Sergio Parisse | Italy | 2002–present | 119 |

* As of June 2016

## FIVE MOST RECENT RUGBY WORLD CUP WINNERS

| YEAR | COUNTRY |
|------|---------|
| 1999 | Australia |
| 2003 | England |
| 2007 | South Africa |
| 2011 | New Zealand |
| 2015 | New Zealand |

## MOST POINTS BY A TEAM IN A SINGLE GAME IN RUGBY WORLD CUP HISTORY

| | |
|---|---|
| 1 | **4 June 1995: New Zealand 145–17 Japan** |
| 2 | 25 October 2003: **Australia** 142–0 Namibia |
| 3 | 2 November 2003: **England** 111–13 Uruguay |
| 4 | 15 September 1995: **New Zealand** 108–13 Portugal |
| 5 | 14 October 1999: **New Zealand** 101–3 Italy |
| 6 | 8 September 2007: **Australia** 91–3 Japan |
| 7 | 18 October 2003: **Australia** 90–8 Romania |
| 8 | 26 May 1995: **Scotland** 89–0 Côte d'Ivoire |
| 9 | 16 September 2007: **France** 87–10 Namibia |
| 10 | 22 September 2011: **South Africa** 87–0 Namibia |

# MOST POINTS SCORED BY AN INDIVIDUAL IN THE RUGBY WORLD CUP*

| | NAME | COUNTRY | POINTS |
|---|---|---|---|
| 1 | **Jonny Wilkinson** | **England** | **277** |
| 2 | Gavin Hastings | Scotland | 227 |
| 3 | Michael Lynagh | Australia | 195 |
| 4 | Daniel Carter | New Zealand | 191 |
| 5 | Grant Fox | New Zealand | 170 |
| 6 | Andrew Mehrtens | New Zealand | 163 |
| 7 | Chris Paterson | Scotland | 140 |
| 8 | Frédéric Michalak | France | 136 |
| 9 | Gonzalo Quesada | Argentina | 135 |
| =10 | Felipe Contepomi | Argentina | 125 |
| =10 | Matt Burke | Australia | 125 |
| =10 | Nicky Little | Fiji | 125 |

* Includes tries, conversions, penalties and drop goals, as of June 2016

# TEN MOST RECENT SIX NATIONS WINNERS

| YEAR | COUNTRY |
|---|---|
| 2007 | France |
| 2008 | Wales |
| 2009 | Ireland |
| 2010 | France |
| 2011 | England |
| 2012 | Wales |
| 2013 | Wales |
| 2014 | Ireland |
| 2015 | Ireland |
| 2016 | England |

# SIX NATIONS WINS

| COUNTRY | NO. OF WINS |
|---|---|
| **France** | **5** |
| **England** | **5** |
| Wales | 4 |
| Ireland | 3 |
| Scotland | 0 |
| Italy | 0 |

# MAJOR TENNIS TOURNAMENTS IN ORDER OF PRIZE MONEY FOR SINGLE PLAYERS*

| 1 | **US Open – $3.5 million (approx. £2.7 million)** |
|---|---|
| 2 | **Australian Open** – AU$3.85 million (approx. £2.25 million) |
| 3 | **Wimbledon** – £2 million |
| 4 | **French Open** – €2.1 million (approx. £1.8 million) |

* As of 2016

# TEN MOST RECENT WIMBLEDON CHAMPIONS (MEN'S AND WOMEN'S SINGLES)

| YEAR | MEN'S CHAMPION | COUNTRY | WOMEN'S CHAMPION | COUNTRY |
|------|----------------|---------|-------------------|---------|
| 2007 | Roger Federer | Switzerland | Venus Williams | USA |
| 2008 | Rafael Nadal | Spain | Venus Williams | USA |
| 2009 | Roger Federer | Switzerland | Serena Williams | USA |
| 2010 | Rafael Nadal | Spain | Serena Williams | USA |
| 2011 | Novak Djokovic | Serbia | Petra Kvitova | Czech Republic |
| 2012 | Roger Federer | Switzerland | Serena Willaims | USA |
| 2013 | Andy Murray | Great Britain | Marion Bartoli | France |
| 2014 | Novak Djokovic | Serbia | Petra Kvitova | Czech Republic |
| 2015 | Novak Djokovic | Serbia | Serena Williams | USA |
| 2016 | Andy Murray | Great Britain | Serena Williams | USA |

# TOP FIVE HIGHEST-EARNING MALE TENNIS PLAYERS*

| 1 | Roger Federer | $97.3 million |
|---|---------------|---------------|
| 2 | Novak Djokovic | $94 million |
| 3 | Rafael Nadal | $75.8 million |
| 4 | Pete Sampras | $43.2 millon |
| 5 | Andy Murray | $42.4 million |

* Total career earnings as of June 2016

# TOP FIVE HIGHEST-EARNING FEMALE TENNIS PLAYERS*

| 1 | Serena Williams | $77.5 million |
|---|-----------------|---------------|
| 2 | Maria Sharapova | $36.5 million |
| 3 | Venus Williams | $33 million |
| 4 | Victoria Azarenka | $28.2 million |
| 5 | Kim Clijsters | $24.4 million |

* Total career earnings as of June 2016

## Fascinating Facts

- The first tennis championships for men were held at Wimbledon in 1877 and 22 players competed in the first year.

- In 1884, the first men's doubles and women's singles were held at Wimbledon.

- The name 'tennis' comes from the French word *tenez*, the imperative form of the verb *tenir* (to hold).

- In 1986, yellow balls were used for the first time in Wimbledon to improve visibility.

- The average person will burn 100 calories in just 14 minutes of tennis.

 # MOST TENNIS GRAND SLAM® WINS (MEN)*

| 1 | Roger Federer | 17 |
|---|---|---|
| =2 | Pete Sampras | 14 |
| =2 | Rafael Nadal | 14 |
| =4 | Novak Djokovic | 12 |
| =4 | Roy Emerson | 12 |
| =6 | Björn Borg | 11 |
| =6 | Rod Laver | 11 |
| 8 | Bill Tilden | 10 |
| =9 | Andre Agassi | 8 |
| =9 | Jimmy Connors | 8 |
| =9 | Ivan Lendl | 8 |
| =9 | Fred Perry | 8 |
| =9 | Ken Rosewall | 8 |

* Tournaments include the Australian Open, French Open, US Open and Wimbledon

## MOST TENNIS GRAND SLAM® WINS (WOMEN)*

| 1 | Margaret Court | 24 |
|---|---|---|
| =2 | Steffi Graf | 22 |
| =2 | Serena Williams | 22 |
| 4 | Helen Wills Moody | 19 |
| =5 | Chris Evert | 18 |
| =5 | Martina Navratilova | 18 |
| 7 | Billie Jean King | 12 |
| =8 | Monica Seles | 9 |
| =8 | Maureen Connolly-Brinker | 9 |
| =10 | Molla Bjurstedt Mallory | 8 |
| =10 | Suzanne Lenglen | 8 |

* Tournaments include the Australian Open, French Open, US Open and Wimbledon

## TOP FIVE MOST CAREER SINGLES TENNIS TITLES (MEN)

| 1 | Jimmy Connors | 109 |
|---|---|---|
| 2 | Ivan Lendl | 94 |
| 3 | Roger Federer | 88 |
| 4 | John McEnroe | 77 |
| 5 | Rafael Nadal | 69 |

# TOP FIVE MOST CAREER SINGLES TENNIS TITLES (WOMEN)

| 1 | Martina Navratilova | 167 |
|---|---|---|
| 2 | Chris Evert | 154 |
| 3 | Steffi Graf | 107 |
| 4 | Margaret Court | 92 |
| 5 | Evonne Goolagong Cawley | 68 |

# TOP FIVE FASTEST RECORDED FIRST SERVES

| | NAME | COUNTRY | SPEED |
|---|---|---|---|
| 1 | Sam Groth | Australia | 163.7 mph (263.4 km/h) |
| 2 | Albano Olivetti | Italy | 160 mph (257.5 km/h) |
| 3 | John Isner | USA | 157.2 mph (253 km/h) |
| =4 | Ivo Karlović | Croatia | 156 mph (251 km/h) |
| =4 | Jerzy Janowicz | Poland | 156 mph (251 km/h) |

# WORLD SNOOKER CHAMPIONS OF THE PAST DECADE

| YEAR | CHAMPION | COUNTRY |
| --- | --- | --- |
| 2007 | John Higgins | Scotland |
| 2008 | Ronnie O'Sullivan | England |
| 2009 | John Higgins | Scotland |
| 2010 | Neil Robertson | Australia |
| 2011 | John Higgins | Scotland |
| 2012 | Ronnie O'Sullivan | England |
| 2013 | Ronnie O'Sullivan | England |
| 2014 | Mark Selby | England |
| 2015 | Stuart Bingham | England |
| 2016 | Mark Selby | England |

## Fascinating Facts

- The fastest frame ever recorded in professional snooker took place on 31 August 1988, when Tony Drago won the fifth frame of his third round in the Fidelity Unit Trusts International match against Danny Fowler in just 3 minutes.

- Ronnie O'Sullivan compiled each of the five fastest 147 breaks ever recorded, the quickest of which took 5 minutes and 20 seconds, recorded in the first round of the 1997 World Championship.

# TEN MOST RECENT GRAND NATIONAL WINNERS

| YEAR | HORSE | JOCKEY | ODDS |
|------|-------|--------|------|
| 2007 | Silver Birch | Robbie Power | 33/1 |
| 2008 | Comply or Die | Timmy Murphy | 7/1 |
| 2009 | Mon Mome | Liam Treadwell | 100/1 |
| 2010 | Don't Push It | Tony McCoy | 25/1 |
| 2011 | Ballabriggs | Jason Maguire | 14/1 |
| 2012 | Neptune Collonges | Daryl Jacob | 33/1 |
| 2013 | Auroras Encore | Ryan Mania | 66/1 |
| 2014 | Pineau de Re | Leighton Aspell | 25/1 |
| 2015 | Many Clouds | Leighton Aspell | 25/1 |
| 2016 | Rule the World | David Mullins | 33/1 |

## Fascinating Fact

- The most valuable racehorse ever was sold in 2006 at the Calder Racecourse. Descended from two Kentucky Derby winners, the colt known as The Green Monkey was bought for $16 million (£10.4 million).

# TEN MOST RECENT RECIPIENTS OF THE BBC SPORTS PERSONALITY OF THE YEAR

| YEAR | SPORTSPERSON | SPORT |
|------|--------------|-------|
| 2006 | Zara Phillips | Equestrian |
| 2007 | Joe Calzaghe | Boxing |
| 2008 | Chris Hoy | Cycling |
| 2009 | Ryan Giggs | Football |
| 2010 | Tony McCoy | Horse Racing |
| 2011 | Mark Cavendish | Cycling |
| 2012 | Bradley Wiggins | Cycling |
| 2013 | Andy Murray | Tennis |
| 2014 | Lewis Hamilton | Formula 1 |
| 2015 | Andy Murray | Tennis |

# TOP TEN TEAMS WITH THE MOST SUPERBOWL WINS

| 1 | Pittsburgh Steelers | 6 |
|------|---------------------|---|
| =2 | San Francisco 49ers | 5 |
| =2 | Dallas Cowboys | 5 |
| =4 | Green Bay Packers | 4 |
| =4 | New York Giants | 4 |
| =4 | New England Patriots | 4 |
| =7 | Denver Bronchos | 3 |
| =7 | Washington Redskins | 3 |
| =7 | Oakland/LA Raiders | 3 |
| =10 | Baltimore/Indianapolis Colts | 2* |

* The Miami Dolphins and the Baltimore Ravens have also won the Superbowl twice

# THEATRE

# TOP TEN LONGEST-RUNNING MUSICALS IN THE WEST END

| 1 | *Les Misérables* – 8 October 1985 to present |
|---|---|
| 2 | *The Phantom of the Opera* – 9 October 1986 to present |
| 3 | *Blood Brothers* – 11 April 1983 to 22 October 1983 and 28 July 1988 to 10 November 2012 |
| 4 | *Cats* – 11 May 1981 to 11 May 2002, 12 December 2014 to 25 April 2015 and 23 October 2015 to 2 January 2016 |
| 5 | *Mamma Mia!* – 6 April 1999 to present |
| 6 | *The Lion King* – 19 October 1999 to present |
| 7 | *Starlight Express* – 27 March 1984 to 12 January 2002 |
| 8 | *Chicago* – 18 November 1997 to 1 September 2012 |
| 9 | *Buddy – The Buddy Holly Story* – 12 October 1989 to 19 May 2002 |
| 10 | *Miss Saigon* – 20 September 1989 to 30 October 1999 and 21 May 2014 to 27 February 2016 |

## Fascinating Fact

- *The Phantom of the Opera* has played to more than 140 million people in 35 countries around the world, with an estimated gross of $6 billion.

# TOP TEN LONGEST-RUNNING SHOWS ON BROADWAY

| | |
|---|---|
| 1 | *The Phantom of the Opera* – **26 January 1988 to present** |
| 2 | *Chicago* (1996 revival) – 14 November 1996 to present |
| 3 | *The Lion King* – 13 November 1997 to present |
| 4 | *Cats* – 7 October 1982 to 10 September 2000 |
| 5 | *Les Misérables* – 12 March 1987 to 18 May 2003 |
| 6 | *A Chorus Line* – 25 July 1975 to 28 April 1990 |
| 7 | *Oh, Calcutta!* – 24 September 1976 to 6 August 1989 |
| 8 | *Mamma Mia!* – 10 October 2001 to 12 September 2015 |
| 9 | *Beauty and the Beast* – 18 April 1994 to 29 July 2007 |
| 10 | *Wicked* – 30 October 2003 to present |

 ACTORS WHO HAVE PLAYED HAMLET

| YEAR | ACTOR | VENUE |
|---|---|---|
| 1937 | Laurence Olivier | Old Vic |
| 1948 | Paul Scofield | Royal Shakespeare Company |
| 1958 | Michael Redgrave | Royal Shakespeare Company |
| 1961 | Ian Bannen | Royal Shakespeare Company |
| 1963 | Peter O'Toole | National Theatre |
| 1964 | Richard Burton | Broadway |
| 1965 | David Warner | Royal Shakespeare Company |

| YEAR | ACTOR | VENUE |
| --- | --- | --- |
| 1975 | Ben Kingsley | Royal Shakespeare Company |
| 1977 | Derek Jacobi | Royal Shakespeare Company |
| 1980 | Jonathan Pryce | Royal Court |
| 1982 | Christopher Walken | American Shakespeare Company |
| 1989 | Ian Charleson | National Theatre |
| 1989 | Mark Rylance | Royal Shakespeare Company |
| 1993 | Kenneth Branagh | Royal Shakespeare Company |
| 1994 | Stephen Dillane | Gielgud Theatre |
| 1995 | Ralph Fiennes | Broadway |
| 2000 | Simon Russell Beale | National Theatre |
| 2001–2 | Samuel West | Royal Shakespeare Company |
| 2004 | Ben Whishaw | Old Vic |
| 2004 | Toby Stephens | Royal Shakespeare Company |
| 2008–9 | David Tennant | Royal Shakespeare Company |
| 2009 | Jude Law | Wyndham's Theatre |
| 2010 | Rory Kinnear | National Theatre |
| 2011 | Michael Sheen | Young Vic |
| 2012 | Michael Benz | Globe Theatre |
| 2015 | Benedict Cumberbatch | National Theatre |

# TEN YEARS OF OLIVIER AWARD WINNERS

| YEAR | BEST ACTRESS | BEST ACTOR |
|---|---|---|
| 2007 | Tamsin Greig *(Much Ado About Nothing)* | Rufus Sewell *(Rock 'n' Roll)* |
| 2008 | Kristin Scott Thomas *(The Seagull)* | Chiwetel Ejiofor *(Othello)* |
| 2009 | Margaret Tyzack *(The Chalk Garden)* | Derek Jacobi *(Twelfth Night)* |
| 2010 | Rachel Weisz *(A Streetcar Named Desire)* | Mark Rylance *(Jerusalem)* |
| 2011 | Nancy Carroll *(After the Dance)* | Roger Allam *(Henry IV)* |
| 2012 | Ruth Wilson *(Anna Christie)* | Benedict Cumberbatch and Jonny Lee Miller *(Frankenstein)* |
| 2013 | Helen Mirren *(The Audience)* | Luke Treadaway *(The Curious Incident of the Dog in the Night-time)* |
| 2014 | Lesley Manville *(Ghosts)* | Rory Kinnear *(Othello)* |
| 2015 | Penelope Wilton *(Taken at Midnight)* | Mark Strong *(A View from the Bridge)* |
| 2016 | Denise Gough *(People, Places and Things)* | Kenneth Cranham *(The Father)* |

# TOP TEN MOST OLIVIER AWARD WINS

|  | NAME | PROFESSION | NO. OF WINS |
|---|---|---|---|
| 1 | **Judi Dench** | **Actress** | **8** |
| 2 | William Dudley | Designer | 7 |
| =3 | Ian McKellen | Actor | 6 |
| =3 | Alan Bennett | Actor/writer | 6 |
| =3 | Richard Eyre | Director | 6 |
| =3 | Stephen Sondheim | Composer | 6 |
| =7 | Matthew Bourne | Choreographer/director | 5 |
| =7 | Declan Donnellan | Director | 5 |
| =7 | Mark Henderson | Lighting designer | 5 |
| =7 | Mark Thompson | Designer | 5 |

# FIVE YEARS OF TONY AWARD WINNERS

| YEAR | ACTOR IN A PLAY | ACTRESS IN A PLAY | ACTOR IN A MUSICAL | ACTRESS IN A MUSICAL |
|---|---|---|---|---|
| 2012 | James Corden (*One Man, Two Guvnors*) | Nina Arianda (*Venus in Fur*) | Steve Kazee (*Once*) | Audra McDonald (*The Gershwins' Porgy and Bess*) |
| 2013 | Tracy Letts (*Who's Afraid of Virginia Woolf?*) | Cicely Tyson (*The Trip to Bountiful*) | Billy Porter (*Kinky Boots*) | Patina Miller (*Pippin*) |

MAN FACTS

| YEAR | ACTOR IN A PLAY | ACTRESS IN A PLAY | ACTOR IN A MUSICAL | ACTRESS IN A MUSICAL |
|---|---|---|---|---|
| 2014 | Bryan Cranston *(All the Way)* | Audra McDonald *(Lady Day at Emerson's Bar and Grill)* | Neil Patrick Harris *(Hedwig and the Angry Inch)* | Jessie Mueller *(Beautiful: The Carole King Musical)* |
| 2015 | Alexander Sharp *(The Curious Incident of the Dog in the Night-time)* | Helen Mirren *(The Audience)* | Michael Cerveris *(Fun Home)* | Kelli O'Hara *(The King and I)* |
| 2016 | Frank Langella *(The Father)* | Jessica Lange *(Long Day's Journey into Night)* | Leslie Odom *(Hamilton)* | Cynthia Erivo *(The Color Purple)* |

## Fascinating Facts

- The earliest documented performance of *Hamlet* took place on board a ship called *The Dragon*, as it lay anchored off the coast of Sierra Leone in 1607. It was staged by the crew to entertain a visiting dignitary.

- Each Olivier Award is a solid bronze statuette weighing 1.6 kilograms. It depicts the young Olivier as *Henry V* at The Old Vic in 1937 and was commissioned by The Society of London Theatre from the sculptor Harry Franchetti.

- David Suchet has been nominated no less than six times, but has never won an Olivier Award.

- The Tony Award is actually named after a woman. 'Toni' was the nickname for Denver actress Antoinette Perry, who later turned successfully to producing and directing.

- Dolores Gray performed the shortest-lived Tony Award-winning role. She won a Tony Award for her performance in *Carnival in Flanders* (1953), a musical that ran for only six performances.

## 🎭 ORIGINS OF THEATRE

Western theatre originated in Ancient Greece. It came out of a state festival in Athens in honour of the god Dionysus. The Athenian city-state exported the festival throughout the Greek world to promote a common identity. The basic structure of the Greek theatre can be recognised in our theatres today.

**Orchestra** – The orchestra (dancing space) was normally circular. It was a level space where the chorus would dance, sing and interact with the actors who were on the stage near the skene. The earliest orchestras were simply made of packed earth but in the Classical period some orchestras began to be paved with marble and other materials. In the centre of the orchestra there was often a thymele (altar).

**Skene** – The skene (tent) was the building directly behind the stage and was usually decorated as a palace, temple or other building, depending on the needs of the play. It had at least one set of doors, and actors could make entrances and exits through them. There was also access to the roof of the skene from behind, so that actors playing gods and other heavenly characters could appear on the roof.

**Theatron** – The theatron (viewing place) was where the spectators sat. The theatron was usually part of a hillside overlooking the orchestra, and often wrapped around a large portion of the orchestra. Spectators in 5 BC probably sat on cushions or boards but by 4 BC the theatron of many Greek theatres had marble seats.

## 🎭 SHAKESPEARE'S PLAYS

| TRAGEDIES |
| --- |
| *Antony and Cleopatra* |
| *Coriolanus* |
| *Hamlet, Prince of Denmark* |
| *Julius Caesar* |
| *King Lear* |

*Macbeth*

*Othello. Moor of Venice*

*Romeo and Juliet*

*Timon of Athens*

*Titus Andronicus*

## HISTORIES

*King John*

*King Richard II*

*King Henry IV, Part One*

*King Henry IV, Part Two*

*King Henry V*

*King Henry VI, Part One*

*King Henry VI, Part Two*

*King Henry VI, Part Three*

*King Richard III*

*King Henry VIII*

## COMEDIES

*All's Well That Ends Well*

*As You Like It*

*The Comedy of Errors*

*Cymbeline*

*Love's Labour's Lost*

*Measure for Measure*

*The Merry Wives of Windsor*

*The Merchant of Venice*

*A Midsummer Night's Dream*

*Much Ado About Nothing*

*Pericles, Prince of Tyre*

*The Taming of the Shrew*

*The Tempest*

*Troilus and Cressida*

*Twelfth Night*

*Two Gentlemen of Verona*

*The Winter's Tale*

# THE SCOTTISH PLAY

Shakespeare's *Macbeth* is considered very bad luck among actors. It is said that there is a history of catastrophes, bad luck and unexplained incidents when the play is performed, and some actors, even today, consider it unlucky to refer to the play by name. Instead, they call *Macbeth* 'the Scottish play'.

As to how this superstition arose is subject to debate. It is that said that the play *Macbeth*, with its witches, spells and incantations, was nervously performed by Shakespeare's actors, and the fear that the play was cursed was confirmed when an actor by the name of Hal Berridge died while playing Lady Macbeth in 1606. Some argue that the superstition was an invention of a later generation of actors.

There is, however, much evidence to support an actor's phobia:

- A dispute between actors and an unappreciative audience member in 1721 turned into a riot, which led to the militia's involvement and the theatre burning down.

- In 1849, another riot in New York during a production was the cause of 23 deaths and injured hundreds.

- In the early 1930s, Dame Lillian Boylis took on the role of Lady Macbeth only to die in the dress rehearsal.

- In 1947, Harold Norman, as Macbeth, was fatally stabbed in the swordfight that ends the play.

- Productions in London's West End in the past 70 years are studded with car crashes, bad theatre-related accidents, sudden deaths and suicide. So perhaps if you do say 'Macbeth', it is best to pay homage to the tradition and leave the room, spin round three times, spit, knock three times and ask to be allowed back in!

# COMMON SHAKESPEARE QUOTES AND THEIR ORIGINS

*'I am a man more sinned against than sinning'*
'Close pent-up guilts / Rive your concealing continents, and cry /
These dreadful summoners grace. I am a man / More sinned against
than sinning'
*King Lear*

*'You've been hoist by your own petard'*
'For 'tis the sport to have the engineer / Hoist with his own petar'*
*Hamlet*
* To cause the engineer to be blown up by his own bomb; that is, to
cause a person to be destroyed by his own deeds. The word 'petar'
is obsolete and is synonymous with 'petard', which is defined as a
pasteboard bomb used in fireworks

*'Love is blind...'*
'But love is blind, and lovers cannot see / The pretty follies that
themselves commit'
*The Merchant of Venice*

# TEN OF THE WORLD'S BEST OPERA HOUSES

Teatro alla Scala (La Scala), Milan, Italy

Opéra de Paris, Paris, France

Sydney Opera House, Sydney, Australia

Royal Opera House, London, UK

Metropolitan Opera House, New York, USA

The Bolshoi, Moscow, Russia

Teatro La Fenice, Venice, Italy

Teatro Colón, Buenos Aires, Argentina

Teatro Real, Madrid, Spain

Wiener Staatsoper, Vienna, Austria

# TRAVEL

# TOP TEN WORLD'S FASTEST AIRCRAFT

| AIRCRAFT | SPEED |
|---|---|
| 1 **X-43A (Unmanned)** | **7,310 mph (11,000 km/h)** |
| 2 X-15 | 4,510 mph (7,258 km/h) |
| 3 Lockheed YF-12 | 2,274 mph (3,661 km/h) |
| 4 SR-71 Blackbird | 2,200 mph (3,540 km/h) |
| 5 MiG-25R Fox bat-B | 2,000 mph (3,219 km/h) |
| 6 X-2 | 1,900 mph (3,058 km/h) |
| 7 XB-70 Valkyrie | 1,890 mph (3,042 km/h) |
| 8 F-15 Eagle | 1,875 mph (3,017 km/h) |
| 9 MiG-31 Foxhound | 1,750 mph (2,816 km/h) |
| 10 F-111 Aardvark | 1,650 mph (2,655 km/h) |

 # TOP TEN AIRCRAFT WITH BIGGEST WINGSPAN

| AEROPLANE | WINGSPAN |
|---|---|
| 1 **Spruce Goose** | **97.6 m (320.1 ft)** |
| 2 AN-225 | 88.7 m (291.1 ft) |
| 3 Airbus A380 | 79.8 m (261.7 ft) |
| 4 AN-214 | 73.3 m (240.5 ft) |
| 5 Convair B-36J Peacemaker | 70.1 m (230.1 ft) |
| 6 Boeing 747-8 | 68.5 m (224.7 ft) |
| 7 C-5 Lockheed Galaxy | 67.9 m (222.8 ft) |
| 8 A350 XWB | 67.7 m (212.4 ft) |
| 9 Boeing 777-200LR | 64.8 m (212.7 ft) |
| 10 Douglas XB-19 | 64.6 m (212 ft) |

# TOP TEN WORLD'S BUSIEST AIRPORTS*

| | AIRPORT | LOCATION | NO. OF PASSENGERS PER MONTH |
|---|---|---|---|
| 1 | Hartsfield–Jackson Atlanta International Airport | Georgia, USA | 101,491,106 |
| 2 | Beijing Capital International Airport | Beijing, China | 89,938,628 |
| 3 | Dubai International Airport | Dubai, United Arab Emirates | 78,014,841 |
| 4 | O'Hare International Airport | Chicago, USA | 76,942,493 |
| 5 | Tokyo International Airport | Tokyo, Japan | 75,316,718 |
| 6 | London Heathrow Airport | London, UK | 74,989,795 |
| 7 | Los Angeles International Airport | California, USA | 74,937,004 |
| 8 | Hong Kong International Airport | Hong Kong, China | 68,283,407 |
| 9 | Charles de Gaulle Airport | Paris, France | 65,766,986 |
| 10 | Dallas / Fort Worth International Airport | Texas, USA | 64,072,468 |

\* Figures indicate total number of passengers in 2015

 **TOP TEN BUSIEST UK AIRPORTS***

| 1 | London Heathrow | 74,985,748 |
|---|---|---|
| 2 | London Gatwick | 40,269,087 |
| 3 | Manchester | 23,136,047 |
| 4 | London Stansted | 22,519,178 |
| 5 | London Luton | 12,263,505 |
| 6 | Edinburgh | 11,114,587 |
| 7 | Birmingham | 10,187,122 |
| 8 | Glasgow International | 8,714,307 |
| 9 | Bristol | 6,786,790 |
| 10 | Newcastle | 4,562,853 |

\* Figures indicate total number of passengers in 2015

 **TOP TEN WORLD'S FASTEST CARS**

| | CAR | MAX SPEED |
|---|---|---|
| 1 | Hennessey Venom GT | 270 mph (435 km/h) |
| 2 | Bugatti Chiron | 261 mph (420 km/h) |
| 3 | SSC Ultimate Aero | 256 mph (412 km/h) |
| 4 | Bugatti Veyron Super Sport | 253 mph (407 km/h) |
| 5 | Koenigsegg CCR | 242 mph (389 km/h) |
| 6 | McLaren F1 | 241 mph (388 km/h) |
| 7 | Aston Martin One-77 | 220 mph (354 km/h) |
| =8 | Jaguar XJ220 | 217 mph (349 km/h) |
| =8 | McLaren P1 | 217 mph (349 km/h) |
| =8 | Ferrari LaFerrari | 217 mph (349 km/h) |

# TOP TEN WORLD'S MOST EXPENSIVE CARS

| 1 | Lamborghini Veneno | £3.47 million ($4.5 million) |
|---|---|---|
| 2 | Lykan Hypersport | £2.6 million ($3.4 million) |
| 3 | Bugatti Veyron Super Sport | £1.85 million ($ 2.4 million) |
| 4 | Aston Martin One-77 | £1.4 million ($1.85 million) |
| 5 | Pagani Zonda Cinque Roadster | £1.4 million ($1.85 million) |
| 6 | Koenigsegg Agera R | £1.23 million ($1.6 million) |
| 7 | McLaren P1 | £1.04 million ($1.35 million) |
| 8 | Pagani Huayra | £1.003 million ($1.3 million) |
| 9 | Zenvo ST1 | £945,763 ($1.225 million) |
| 10 | Hennessey Venom GT Spyder | £870,000 ($1.1 million) |

 # TOP TEN BIGGEST CAR MANUFACTURING COUNTRIES

| | COUNTRY | NO. OF UNITS MANUFACTURED IN 2015 |
|---|---|---|
| 1 | China | 24,503,326 |
| 2 | USA | 12,100,095 |
| 3 | Japan | 9,278,238 |
| 4 | Germany | 6,033,164 |
| 5 | South Korea | 4,555,957 |
| 6 | India | 4,125,744 |
| 7 | Mexico | 3,565,469 |
| 8 | Spain | 2,733,201 |
| 9 | Brazil | 2,429,463 |
| 10 | Canada | 2,283,474 |

# NUMBER OF CARS PRODUCED GLOBALLY OVER THE PAST DECADE

| YEAR | UNITS PRODUCED |
| --- | --- |
| 2006 | 49,918,578 |
| 2007 | 53,201,346 |
| 2008 | 52,726,117 |
| 2009 | 47,772,598 |
| 2010 | 58,264,852 |
| 2011 | 59,929,016 |
| 2012 | 63.069,541 |
| 2013 | 65,140,268 |
| 2014 | 67,782,035 |
| 2015 | 68,539,516 |

# TOP TEN COUNTRIES WITH THE DEADLIEST ROADS

| | COUNTRY | ROAD TRAFFIC DEATHS PER 100,000 OF THE POPULATION |
| --- | --- | --- |
| 1 | **Namibia** | **45** |
| 2 | Thailand | 44 |
| 3 | Iran | 38 |
| =4 | Sudan | 36 |
| =4 | Swaziland | 36 |
| 6 | Venezuala | 35 |
| 7 | Congo | 34 |
| =8 | Malawi | 32 |
| =8 | Dominican Republic | 32 |
| =8 | Iraq | 32 |

# TOP TEN WORLD'S BUSIEST SEA PORTS*

| 1 | Shanghai, China | 35.29 |
|---|---|---|
| 2 | Singapore | 33.87 |
| 3 | Shenzhen, China | 24.03 |
| 4 | Hong Kong, China | 22.23 |
| 5 | Ningbo-Zhoushan, China | 19.45 |
| 6 | Busan, South Korea | 18.65 |
| 7 | Qingdao, China | 16.62 |
| 8 | Guangzhou, China | 16.16 |
| 9 | Jebel Ali, Dubai, UAE | 15.25 |
| 10 | Tianjin, China | 14.05 |

\* Figures indicate how many TEUs (20-foot equivalent units) in their millions were handled in 2014

## Fascinating Fact

- Portholes are traditionally round because the constant up and down motion of a ship places a lot of strain and stress on a ship's outer covering. If portholes were designed at angles, the stress would tend to concentrate at those points and crack the outer covering. As portholes are circular, this stress is evenly distributed around the holes, making it less likely for these cracks to occur.

# TEN OF THE MOST FAMOUS SHIPS THROUGHOUT HISTORY

1. **RMS *Titanic* – The *Titanic*, on her maiden voyage, struck an iceberg in the North Atlantic and sank with the loss of 1,513 lives on 15 April 1912. She was, at the time, the world's largest passenger liner and considered unsinkable.**

2. **HMS *Victory*** – Nelson's flagship. Nelson died from a bullet wound on the ship's deck during the Battle of Trafalgar, 21 October 1805.

3. ***Mayflower*** – The ship that transported the pilgrims from Plymouth, England, to Plymouth Colony, Massachusetts, USA, in 1620.

4. **HMS *Endeavour*** – The ship in which Captain James Cook claimed Australia for Britain during his first voyage (1768–71).

5. **HMS *Bounty*** – *Bounty* was involved in the most famous mutiny in naval history in 1789. Captain William Bligh and 18 of his crew were set adrift in the Pacific, but they survived and safely reached Timor. The mutineers, led by Fletcher Christian, settled on Pitcairn Island, where their ancestors still live today.

6. ***Mary Rose*** – Henry VIII's greatest warship, which sank off Southsea in 1545. She was recovered in 1982 and her remains are on display at Portsmouth.

7. ***Marie Celeste*** – An American brigantine found deserted in the Atlantic in 1872 with absolutely no crew. The abandonment is a great mystery, as the cargo was intact and the saloon cabin was laid for tea.

8. **HMS *Beagle*** – Carried a young Charles Darwin on its five-year voyage via South America and its islands, leading to the publication of *On the Origin of Species* in 1859.

9. ***Niña*, *Pinta* and *Santa Maria*** – The fleet sailed by Christopher Columbus to the West Indies, the discovery of which opened up the New World in 1492.

10. ***Rainbow Warrior*** – The international protest ship belonging to Greenpeace, the environmental action group, was badly damaged by two explosions while moored in New Zealand in July 1985.

 # THE SHIPPING FORECAST

The shipping forecast is regularly broadcast for the sea areas around the British Isles. From the north of Scotland clockwise, these are the areas:

| | |
|---|---|
| South-east Iceland | Dover |
| Faeroes | Wight |
| Fair Isle | Portland |
| Viking | Plymouth |
| North Utsire | Biscay |
| South Utsire | FitzRoy |
| Cromarty | Sole |
| Forties | Lundy |
| Forth | Irish Sea |
| Dogger | Fastnet |
| Tyne | Shannon |
| Humber | Rockall |
| Fisher | Malin |
| German Bight | Hebrides |
| Thames | Bailey |

 # TOP FIVE FASTEST TRAINS IN SERVICE IN THE WORLD

| | NAME | COUNTRY | MAX. SPEED |
|---|---|---|---|
| 1 | **Shanghai Maglev** | **China** | **268 mph (431 km/h)** |
| 2 | Harmony CRH 380A | China | 236 mph (380 km/h) |
| 3 | AGV Italo | Italy | 223 mph (360 km/h) |
| =4 | Velaro E | Spain | 217 mph (350 km/h) |
| =4 | Talgo 350 | Spain | 217 mph (350 km/h) |

## Fascinating Fact

- A Japanese maglev train set the world speed record for a manned, railed vehicle when it hit 374 mph (603 km/h) in April 2015 during trials.

# TEN OF THE MOST FAMOUS TRAINS IN HISTORY

1. ***Orient Express*** – The two city names most intimately associated with the *Orient Express* are Paris and Istanbul, whereas the modern regular scheduled train that bears the name now serves neither. The current *Orient Express* runs from Strasbourg to Vienna, leaving Strasbourg at 10.20 p.m. daily.

2. ***Flying Scotsman*** – This passenger train has run between London, England, and Edinburgh, Scotland, since 1862. The service is currently operated by Virgin Trains East Coast.

3. **Trans-Siberian Railway** – This is a network of railways connecting Moscow and European Russia with the Russian Far East provinces, Mongolia, China and the Sea of Japan. It was built between 1891 and 1916, and is 5,772 miles (9,288 km) long. It spans eight time zones and takes about seven days to complete its journey.

4. **Burma Railway** – Also known as the 'Death Railway', it is a 258-mile (415-km) railway between Bangkok, Thailand and Rangoon, Myanmar (Burma), built by the Empire of Japan during World War Two to support its forces in the Burma campaign. Forced labour was used in its construction and over 100,000 Asian labourers and 16,000 Allied POWs died as a direct result of the project.

5  *Glacier Express* – Running from Zermatt to St Moritz in Switzerland, this train is not an express in the high-speed sense of the term, but rather that it provides a one-seat ride from end to end (even though the train travels over several different railroad lines). It is a 7½-hour railway journey across 291 bridges, through 91 tunnels and across the Oberalp Pass at 2,033 m in altitude.

6  *Blue Train* – This train travels a 1,000-mile (1,600-km) journey between Pretoria and Cape Town in South Africa. It is one of the most luxurious train journeys in the world.

7  *20th Century Limited* – An express passenger train operated by the New York Central Railroad from 1902 to 1967, during which time it became the 'Most Famous Train in the World'. Known for its speed as well as for its style, passengers walked to and from the train on a plush, crimson carpet, which was rolled out at station stops, thus the 'red-carpet treatment' was born.

8  *Ghan* – This is the 48-hour, 2,979-km passenger train travelling from Adelaide, through Alice Springs, to Darwin. The service's name is an abbreviated version of its previous nickname 'The Afghan Express', which comes from the Afghan camel trains that trekked the same route before the advent of the railway.

9  *Rheingold Express* – This legendary train travelled between Hoek van Holland near Rotterdam and Basel, Switzerland, a distance of 662 km. Its operation ended in 1987 after 59 years and 15 days.

10  *Brighton Belle* – This Pullman service ran from 1934, between London's Victoria Station and Brighton on the Sussex coast, until its withdrawal from service on 20 April 1972.

## Fascinating Fact

- The London Underground was the world's first underground railway when it opened on 10 January 1863. It is also the world's longest underground with 250 miles (402 km) of track. Each year, a typical Tube train travels around 114,500 miles (184,270 km).

# TOP FIVE WORLD'S FASTEST ROAD MOTORCYCLES

| | NAME | MAX. SPEED |
|---|---|---|
| **1** | **MTT Turbine Y2K Superbike** | **227 mph (402 km/h)** |
| 2 | Lightning LS-218 | 218 mph (350 km/h) |
| 3 | Ducati Panigale 1199 R | 200 mph (321 km/h) |
| 4 | Suzuki Hayabusa | 194 mph (312 km/h) |
| 5 | BMW S1000RR | 190 mph (305 km/h) |

## Fascinating Facts

- The longest motorbike ride through a tunnel of fire was achieved in September 2014 in Parys, South Africa, at a record 120 m (395 ft).

- The tallest rideable motorbike was made in Italy, and is 5.10 m (16 ft 8 in) tall. It is powered by a 5.7-litre V8 engine, running at 280 hp.

- The record for the longest backwards motorcycle ride is 125.5 miles (202 km) and was achieved in Jabalpur, India, on 7 October 2014.

# TOP TEN WORLD'S MOST POPULAR TOURIST DESTINATIONS

| | COUNTRY | INTERNATIONAL TOURIST ARRIVALS IN 2015 |
|---|---|---|
| 1 | **France** | **83.7 million** |
| 2 | USA | 74.8 million |
| 3 | Spain | 65 million |
| 4 | China | 55.6 million |
| 5 | Italy | 48.6 million |
| 6 | Turkey | 39.8 million |
| 7 | Germany | 33 million |
| 8 | UK | 32.6 million |
| 9 | Russia | 29.8 million |
| 10 | Mexico | 29.1 million |

## Fascinating Fact

- The world's fastest elevator, in the Shanghai Tower, China's tallest building, boasts a maximum speed of 1,230 metres per minute, or 73.8 kilometres per hour.

# TOP TEN LARGEST HOTELS IN THE WORLD*

| | |
|---|---|
| 1 | **MGM Grand, Las Vegas: 6,852 rooms. Best feature: a 1000-foot-long pool.** |
| 2 | **First World Hotel**, Malaysia: 6,118 rooms. Best feature: an indoor theme park. |
| 3 | **Disney's All-Star Hotel**, Orlando: 5,524 rooms. Best feature: being able to watch Disney films by the Surfboard Bay Pool. |
| 4 | **Izmailovo Hotel**, Moscow: 5,000 rooms. Best feature: modern infrastructure makes it a 'city within the city'. |
| 5 | **Wynn**, Las Vegas: 4,750 rooms. Best feature: the hotel is full of art. |
| 6 | **Luxor,** Las Vegas: 4,408 rooms. Best feature: the hotel is in the shape of a pyramid and has a replica of the tomb of Tutankhamun. |
| 7 | **Ambassador City Jomtien Hotel**, Thailand: 4,219 rooms. Best feature: situated on a coastline known for its windsailing and surfing opportunities. |
| 8 | **Venetian Hotel**, Las Vegas: 4,024 rooms. Best feature: includes a river and gondolas. |
| 9 | **Excalibur**, Las Vegas: 4,008 rooms. Best feature: medieval-style architecture. |
| 10 | **Aria Resort and Casino**, Las Vegas: 4,004 rooms. Best feature: illuminated with a multitude of colours. |

*As of 2015

# TOP TEN MOST VISITED CITIES IN THE WORLD

| 1 | Hong Kong | China |
|---|---|---|
| 2 | London | UK |
| 3 | Singapore | Singapore |
| 4 | Bangkok | Thailand |
| 5 | Paris | France |
| 6 | Macau | China |
| 7 | Shenzhen | China |
| 8 | New York City | USA |
| 9 | Istanbul | Turkey |
| 10 | Kuala Lumpur | Malaysia |

# TOP TEN MOST VISITED TOURIST ATTRACTIONS IN THE WORLD

| | PLACE | LOCATION | NO. OF VISITORS IN 2014 |
|---|---|---|---|
| 1 | Las Vegas Strip | Nevada, USA | 39.6 million |
| 2 | Times Square | NYC, USA | 39.2 million |
| 3 | Central Park | NYC, USA | 37.5 million |
| 4 | Union Station | Washington, D. C., USA | 32.85 million |
| 5 | Niagra Falls | Ontario, Canada | 22.5 million |
| 6 | Grand Central Terminal | NYC, USA | 21.6 million |

| 7 | Faneuil Hall Marketplace | Boston, USA | 18 million |
|---|---|---|---|
| 8 | Disneyworld's Magic Kingdom | Orlando, USA | 17.5 million |
| 9 | Disneyland Park | Anaheim, USA | 15.9 million |
| 10 | Forbidden City | Beijing, China | 15.3 million |

# TOP TEN MOST VISITED MUSEUMS IN THE WORLD

|  | MUSEUM | PLACE | NO. OF VISITORS PER YEAR* |
|---|---|---|---|
| 1 | **Musée du Louvre** | **Paris, France** | **9,300,000** |
| 2 | National Museum of China | Beijing, China | 7,600,000 |
| 3 | National Museum of Natural History | Washington, USA | 7,300,000 |
| =4 | National Air and Space Museum | Washington, USA | 6,700,000 |
| =4 | British Museum | London, UK | 6,700,000 |
| 6 | National Gallery | London, UK | 6,400,000 |
| 7 | Metropolitan Museum of Art | New York City, USA | 6,300,000 |
| 8 | Vatican Museums | Vatican City, Italy | 6,200,000 |
| 9 | Tate Modern | London, UK | 5,800,000 |
| 10 | National Palace Museum | Taipei, Taiwan | 5,400,000 |

* Attendance in 2014

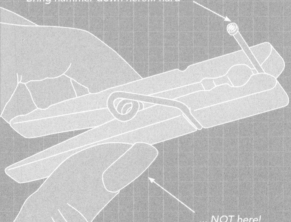

# LIFE HACKS

## Handy Hints to Make Life Easier

*Bring hammer down here... hard*

*... NOT here!*

Dan Marshall

Over **130** amazing hacks inside!

# LIFE HACKS
## Handy Hints to Make Life Easier

Dan Marshall

ISBN: 978 1 84953 644 8          £9.99          Paperback

**EVER ACCIDENTALLY USED YOUR THUMB AS A HAMMER CUSHION WHILE PARTAKING IN A SPOT OF DIY?**

**DO YOU BECOME ENRAGED AT THE UNCONTROLLABLE BOBBING OF THE STRAW IN YOUR DRINKS CAN?**

**ARE YOU YEARNING TO FIND A WAY TO MAKE YOUR TOILET ROLL TUBE ENHANCE YOUR MUSIC LISTENING EXPERIENCE?**

These and dozens of other everyday dilemmas are solved with LIFE HACKS, your handy guide to tackling little annoyances before they turn into big problems. This fully illustrated manual covers everything from nifty electric cable management to ingenious cooking methods and much, much, more.

**Remember: if life throws you a curveball – HACK IT!**

# BIKE PORN: Volume 1

Chris Naylor

ISBN: 978 1 84953 481 9       £14.99       Hardback

## ALL BIKES ARE BEAUTIFUL, BUT SOME ARE DOWNRIGHT SEXY.

BIKE PORN brings together stunning photographs of some of the most seductive and tantalising bikes ever made, from the slickest single-speeds to the most teched-out racing machines and beyond, captured in all their finely crafted glory.

# BIKE PORN: Mountain Bikes

Chris Naylor

ISBN: 978 1 84953 743 8       £14.99       Hardback

## ALL MOUNTAIN BIKES ARE MADE FOR THE GREAT OUTDOORS, BUT SOME ARE MADE FOR GREATNESS.

This seductive selection of photographs and inspirational words brings together close-ups, full body shots and thrilling action, from mountain biking's hottest rigids, hardtails and full suspensions. For all those who love getting dirty with their bikes.

Have you enjoyed this book?
If so, why not write a review on your favourite website?

If you're interested in finding out more about our books, find us on
Facebook at **Summersdale Publishers** and follow us on
Twitter at **@Summersdale**.

Thanks very much for buying this Summersdale book.

## www.summersdale.com